UNDER THE SICKLE AND THE SLEDGEHAMMER

UNDER THE SICKLE AND THE SLEDGEHAMMER

ONE WOMAN'S PRIVATE DIARY FROM 1930s SOVIET RUSSIA

KIRSTI HUURRE

TRANSLATED AND EDITED BY ANNA HYRSKE

First published 1942 as *Sirpin ja moukarin alla*, by Werner Söderström Osakeyhtiö

First published in the English Language, 2024

The History Press
97 St George's Place, Cheltenham,
Gloucestershire, GL50 3QB
www.thehistorypress.co.uk

© Kirsti Huurre, 1942, 2024
Edit and English-language translation © Anna Hyrske, 2024

The right of Kirsti Huurre to be identified as the Author of this work has been asserted in accordance with the Copyright, Designs and Patents Act 1988.

All rights reserved. No part of this book may be reprinted or reproduced or utilised in any form or by any electronic, mechanical or other means, now known or hereafter invented, including photocopying and recording, or in any information storage or retrieval system, without the permission in writing from the Publishers.

British Library Cataloguing in Publication Data.
A catalogue record for this book is available from the British Library.

ISBN 978 1 80399 669 1

Typesetting and origination by The History Press
Printed and bound in Great Britain by TJ Books Limited, Padstow, Cornwall.

Contents

Introduction by Anna Hyrske   7
Author's Preface, 1942   13
Maps   14

1	8 October 1932	17
2	9 October 1932	21
3	10 October 1932	27
4	Late October 1932	31
5	November 1932	35
6	February to Summer 1933	37
7	Summer to Autumn 1933	43
8	October 1933	45
9	Summer 1933 to Christmas 1933	47
10	Christmas Eve 1933	51
11	January to May 1934	57
12	Spring 1934	63
13	Summer 1934	69
14	Autumn 1934	73
15	January 1935	77
16	Spring 1935	81
17	Summer 1935	87
18	August 1935	93

19	Mid-October 1935	97
20	Mid to Late October 1935	103
21	Late October 1935	107
22	December 1935	111
23	January 1936	123
24	March 1936	129
25	Spring 1936 to Autumn 1937	135
26	Autumn 1937	141
27	Summer 1938	147
28	Autumn 1938	155
29	Late 1938 to Late 1939	161
30	November 1939	169
31	Winter 1939	175
32	March 1940	181
33	Summer to Autumn 1940	187
34	Spring to Summer 1941	195
35	Summer 1941	201
36	Late Summer 1941	209
37	August 1941	219

Epilogue by Anna Hyrske   223

Introduction
by Anna Hyrske

Under the Sickle and the Sledgehammer (*Sirpin ja moukarin alla*) was originally published in 1942, as war was still raging between Finland and the Soviet Union, the outcome still unknown. (Finland was to remain independent but at the price of losing vast areas.) Subsequently, in 1944, with the Allied Control Commission (ACC) making demands on the Finnish government across a number of areas, the book fell victim to a rigorous Soviet-led censorship of literature. The ACC was controlled by its 150–200 Soviet members (Britain, for example, had only fifteen seats); in official communications its name was often displayed as 'Allied (Soviet) Commission', highlighting where the supremacy lay.

The Commission began its work in September 1944, and it lost no time in rolling out its book censorship programme. By October that year, publishers, bookstores and libraries had been contacted with the aim of curbing access to literature that could be considered detrimental to relations between the two countries.

A list of around 300 proscribed titles, *Under the Sickle and the Sledgehammer* among them, was distributed to Finnish bookshops; the books were to be removed from the shelves and returned to publishers. Libraries across the country also received letters to demand the withdrawal of titles that might have been damaging to Soviet–Finnish relations, but it did not specify any titles: librarians had to judge for themselves. According to Kai Ekholm's *The Banned Books of 1944–1946*, a PhD thesis published in 2000, the range and quantity of books varied significantly between libraries: most libraries withdrew books in their dozens whereas the Helsinki City Library removed 4,000 volumes. Ekholm's research reveals that *Under the Sickle and the Sledgehammer* was banned by 267 local governments during those years (out of around 400 at the time), second only to Adolf Hitler's *Mein Kampf*, which was deemed unacceptable in 292 localities. It wasn't until 1958 that researchers had access to the book, but only by asking a librarian to fetch it from the so-called 'poison cabinet' – the name given to a locked cabinet housing literature perceived as too dangerous for general consumption. I have seen copies containing an inscription made by the Finnish military in 1942–43: apparently, the book was awarded as a prize for outstanding achievement, presumably on account of its potential to further encourage anti-Soviet sentiment, which goes a long way to explain why the Soviet Commission was so keen to blacklist it.

Under the Sickle and the Sledgehammer starts in 1932, seven years before the Winter War was to erupt and fourteen years after the Finnish Civil War. Finland had gained its independence peacefully from Russia in 1917, in the aftermath of the October Revolution and the downfall of Imperial Russia. The proletariat in Russia had enough to do maintaining stability within their own borders, and Finland seized the opportunity. For a little over 100 years prior to its independence, Finland – or rather the Grand Duchy of Finland – had been an autonomous state within the Russian Empire with its own currency and legislative structures. And for several hundred years before 1809, which marked the end of the Finnish War between Sweden and Russia, Finland had been part of Sweden.

Although Finland didn't actually fight Russia for its independence, that is not to say the transition from Grand Duchy to an independent state didn't involve bloodshed. Less than two months after the declaration of independence, civil war broke out between the 'Reds' and the

Introduction by Anna Hyrske

'Whites'. Finland had undergone massive social change – population growth, urbanisation, resettlement – and these destabilising trends, coupled with the impacts of the power struggles of World War I, led to two polarised forces fighting for supremacy. The Reds represented a socialist world view and wanted the government to be formed by one proletarian party; the Whites had no common political view other than opposition to communism and socialism. The Whites were better equipped and had a greater number of professional combatants, and this afforded them the upper hand in war conditions. The Civil War was brutal – especially for the Reds. Casualty numbers in conflict were similar on both sides, but the Reds also suffered major losses through executions, deaths in captivity and those 'missing in action'. Some reports claim that 12,500 Red lives were lost within prison camps compared with a White toll of merely four. This goes some way to explain the rawness of feelings – the emotional and physical wounds – within Finnish society in the early 1930s, with many of the crimes of the Civil War left unpunished. Indeed, the Civil War and its aftermath very likely acted as a catalyst for the effectiveness of Soviet propaganda promising a better life, better jobs and better housing across the border. Throughout this book we encounter characters who have traversed that border, and, as often as not, the question is asked: did they arrive legitimately or did they use clandestine means? The conversations we hear in this book suggest that many of those travelling without a passport had been previously interned in one of these prison camps. Kaarina herself, the narrator of this story, tells of having occasionally visited a friend in such a place. Others had apparently spent time in hospitals in conjunction with their term in a camp, the implication consistently being that conditions in the camps were harsh. This is a highly plausible motivation for wanting to find a more equitable place to live.

Despite having friends who fought against the Whites, and despite being intrigued by the proletariat movement in Russia, Kaarina was not active within the Reds; nor was her family. On the contrary, her father was a businessman with dozens of employees and a centrally located store selling tailor-made men's and women's clothing. Interestingly, the Helsinki city-centre building where he ran his business is today the home of a Louis Vuitton store. Kaarina's first husband, and father of her son Poju, had a butcher's shop in central Helsinki. He was not a communist supporter, so her interest in the utopia of a workers' paradise must have been fuelled by outside influences, such as pamphlets, adverts, meetings and conversations with those who had already crossed the border or were planning to cross.

I have been aware of this story since my late teenage years because it was written by my great-grandmother. She is the Kaarina and the narrator of this harrowing tale, although for good reason she published under the pseudonym Kirsti Huurre (all the names in the story have been anonymised). The Poju in the story is my grandfather, and he is still alive. I have had the opportunity on a few occasions to talk to him about his mother's life choices and their outcomes. He read the original version at some point in his life, but only once. He agreed without hesitation to my suggestion of translating and editing it. To him, though, it is simply part of his own life story, and he finds it intriguing that others might be interested in it! I never had the chance to meet my great-great-grandfather (Kaarina's father in Helsinki) but I have some pictures of me as a baby with my great-great-grandmother. My great-grandmother Kaarina remained a distant character, living out the remaining years of her life in Sweden for fear of being deported from Finland as a Soviet citizen.

I have been toying with the idea of translating this story into English for a very long time because I believe it's a story worth sharing. But it was the Russian invasion of Ukraine in February 2022 that propelled me into action, convincing me that this story really needs to be retold and brought to light once again. The Russian approach of vilifying its neighbours, the fake information used to justify an attack – it is all disconcertingly reminiscent of what happened in the 1930s. Then, just as now, it's the general population – the ordinary people – who suffer from the decisions made by people clinging to power. My great-grandmother took at face

Introduction by Anna Hyrske

value the narrative that was being circulated by some Finns or their Soviet comrades: power is in the hands of the working class, access to fulfilling work and good-quality housing for all, and your role in society is not determined by money or family background. By the time she'd seen through all the layers of propaganda, it was too late. In the book she conveys how the Russians ardently believed in this 'freedom' as something to strive for, but in the face of all the evidence still failed to realise that it was no such thing. Those who had imigrated to Soviet Russia from abroad, such as Americans or her fellow Finns, were able to take a more objective view and make comparisons with what they had left behind.

A modern English-speaking reader can at times feel quite distant from the book's original Finnish audience, both historically and geographically. In acknowledgement of this, I have added a few footnotes where I thought an explanation might help. There are many place names, which as well as being potentially unfamiliar, have both Russian and Finnish forms. Even the book's title requires some explanation. It is not 'the hammer and sickle', the customary emblem of the Soviet Union, but rather a deliberate play on this: the word 'sledgehammer' was chosen to emphasise the violence, force and power exerted over members of the population who didn't fit into the mould, came from the wrong background, or dared to voice their opinions, even about the most trivial issues. To help readers locate the events in the book, there are maps on pages 14–15. This also offers an overview of the physical distances involved in Kaarina's travels – although bear in mind they were not always achieved at the speed we might expect today, as evidenced by a 250km train journey that lasted a week!

I am pleased that, over eighty years after its original publication, my great-grandmother's first-person testimony will finally reach an English-speaking audience. I believe it's a valuable voice that should be heard, bringing more detail and experience to debates about government propaganda and violence, and the importance of free speech and media.

The opinions stated here are my own and mine alone. They do not reflect the views of my past, current or future employers. The rest of the book is the voice of Kaarina – how she experienced changes in society and the prevailing mood as war approached. With my translation and editing, I feel I have done justice to Kaarina's writing, ably assisted by Dean Bargh from Witchwood Production House, without whom this project could not have succeeded.

Anna Hyrske, Helsinki
March 2023

Author's Preface, 1942

This book is no spur-of-the-moment thing. It evolved as my life evolved in the nine years I endured living in Soviet Russia.

Most of the people in this book appear under pseudonyms because, so long as we still await a major resolution, I don't have the right to betray their faith and jeopardise my unfortunate friends still trapped on the other side of the Soviet border. In addition, there are many families in Finland who are not yet ready to share in public the suffering of their loved ones.

My intention in writing this isn't as propaganda to warn any Finns who might still be entertaining dreams about the sledgehammer and the sickle. I simply want to provide an honest account of what my friends and I had to live through under the 'Stalinist sun'.

The Author, Olonets
28 February 1942

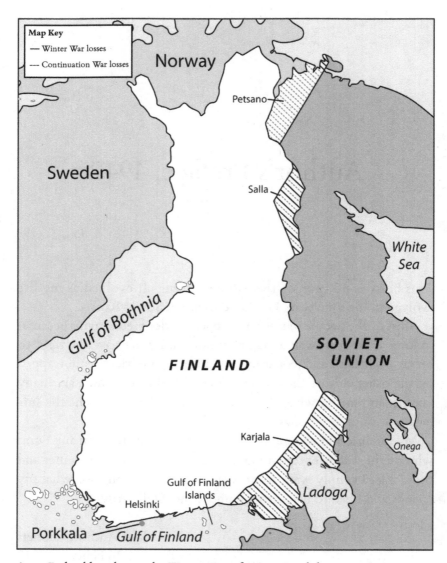

Areas Finland lost during the Winter War of 1939–40 and the Continuation War of 1941–44.

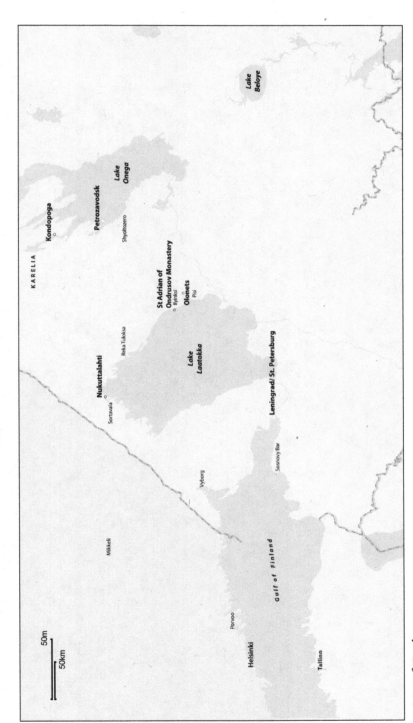

Map of Karelia.

1

8 October 1932

So now here it was at last. The awful act of abandoning that I had been dreading for weeks and never ever really wanted to happen. But it had to be. I had forced myself to go down this path. So I couldn't just leave silently, like a thief in the night, no word of goodbye.

Besides, we didn't have to be apart for long – me and Poju,[1] my little bright-eyed love, who had watched in wonder as I made my week-long preparations. Whatever must that little man be thinking about all this? But perhaps it would have been wiser to take him with me rather than leave him with my parents? Although that would have hurt my mother and father probably more than anything I'd done before. The boy meant the world to them, especially my mother, for whom he was the only fixed point in her life. And even if my own right as a mother to be with Poju was undeniable, it was equally undeniable that I shouldn't be dragging Poju out of this loving environment, where he had spent his whole life. And it was far from certain how soon I would get everything in order in my new circumstances – how soon I would be standing on my own two feet and be able to give him the equivalent of what my parents could give him. This was also the way my relatives saw it. Altogether, it was probably the wisest course of action. Only the future will tell. The date today is 8 October 1932.

---

1   *Poju* means 'My boy'.

The light in the second carriage was rather dim. I couldn't read, and sleep was out of the question. As the memories darted about here and there like distressed winter sparrows, my tears kept welling up, filling my eyes every now and again and blinding me. Poju's eyes seemed to be staring at me from every wall, even as night fell. But, dispassionately and steadily, the iron horse devoured one kilometre after another, taking me farther and farther away from my loved ones.

From time to time, I allowed myself to think that it was just one of those bad dreams that foretell a terrible future. But no! I really had mercilessly parted company with my boy and fled my homeland. This journey was taking me to a new country, a new world, whose beautiful purple colours were reflected all around, making the hearts of the workers beat faster, harder and bolder. I was on my way to a country where power lay in the hands of workers, not money, privilege or ruthlessness, a country where you could be free and happy. For the sake of this country, how many of my comrades had defied the night, the sea and the bitter cold, braced themselves for the struggle, and left behind a relatively good life in their homeland, quietly heading in search of the values and the kind of life they had always dreamt about? Several of them had found themselves unemployed, or were enduring some other hardship, and that made it easier for them to see this displacement as the answer; and some of them had been smuggled across the border in suspicious circumstances.

But what about me? It wasn't external forces or necessity that were driving me away. There was nothing at home that I could point to and say that was the reason. But neither was I was one of those fortunate ones whose path was laid out before them. I had simply been listening to those stirring words and seen in my mind the picture that had been so skilfully painted for me, my eyes wide with excitement. I desperately wanted to *be there*, too. And, once I had made up my mind, nothing could stop me from going. My life was so flat, so colourless, so it was downright madness to stay when I had the opportunity to leave. My boy was the only anchor. 'What should I do? What should I do?' The words hissed in my ears incessantly. After many sleepless nights, I finally resolved it. For now – and only for now – I would

8 October 1932

leave him with my parents until I had managed to get my life organised and I could come and get him or send for him. This all played in my mind repeatedly as I leant back on the soft carriage seat, alone and miserable. Not that I wasn't aware of my fellow travellers. I was surprised to find only two others in the carriage with me: two men. One was leaning casually against the wall, feet up on the edge of the bench opposite. A little further away, a blond gentleman was sitting diagonally across, trying to read his newspaper. Every now and then, I saw him looking inquisitively at my attempt to fight back my tears. A suspicion flashed across my mind that he might be one of the escorts that the police department (or so it was rumoured) deployed for everyone travelling to the Soviet Union. For some reason, the thought felt so childish that I dismissed it straight away. What could they possibly expect to achieve with something like that? It was a silly idea, just like that funny situation at the train station as I was leaving. Someone I knew had pulled me aside and somewhat nervously exclaimed that a representative of the state police, a man in a bowler hat, had also come to see me off. This had seemed strangely exciting, so I asked my acquaintance to discreetly point out the uninvited escort. And what do you know, my friend walks behind my dear unsuspecting father and then waves clumsily, signalling to me. Poor Daddy, not saying a word – and of course upset by our impending separation – had been standing a little way from me, nervously prodding his walking stick here and there. I laughed to see my 'informant' and was amused by his embarrassment.

The thought passed. Have I ever spent such a miserable night? It dragged on so slowly, my heart pumping and my nerves straining. I greeted the first morning with eyes still open, dry lips, and a throbbing temple. It was a relief when I could actually see something emerging in the gradually brightening landscape. Soon the forests were running along the side of the track, in yellows and reds shining in the peaceful Sunday morning sun. I got out for a walk at Vyborg Station. In a restaurant that looked like a ballroom, I had a coffee, and it felt like I was drinking something historically significant. It depressed me at first, but at least the coffee relieved my headache.

Rajajoki![2] Was that Rajajoki? How unimportant it looked, and how much of a dividing line it was all the same, separating two completely different worlds. How many had crossed it, closing all the doors behind them, burning their bridges in pursuit of happiness? Would I find my happiness and fortune after I'd crossed it, or was it written in the stars that my path would be one of pain and suffering? Just like it always had been. A sequence of events swept rapidly through my mind like an old film, depicting so much: my short and bitter marriage, a time in my life which had only one good thing in it – my boy. Everything else I wanted to forget. Dear boy, whom I – crazy, crazy, crazy me – dared to leave behind! I wished I could turn back right now, go home again, wrap my little loved one in my arms, and whisper a thousand silly things in his little ear, things that only a mother and her child can understand.

---

2   The Finnish word for the River Sestra – literal translation is Border River.

2

9 October 1932

But it was too late now. Rajajoki, the river that marked the border, had been crossed. My eyes puffy, I looked out, and the numbness subsided as my interest stirred.

For today was a Sunday, and it had been the same familiar tableau at every Finnish station: people in their Sunday best passing the time by watching the trains come in and seeing who was getting off. Everyone glowing with their customary Sunday tranquillity. But here it immediately looked different: a couple of men on either end of a strange saw, each pulling back and forth. It would take me a while to get used to the Soviet weekly schedule.

I survived Customs without much difficulty, for which I could thank my dear father, who had vehemently opposed excessive hand luggage. In trepidation, I followed the man to whom I had given my passport. I found myself in a small room in which a soldier with very stern eyes seemed to view me as the enemy, to judge by his attitude. He demanded I show him the contents of my handbag, and reveal all those vain, superfluous items you find in a woman's bag. There was no sign of any softening in his eyes when he inspected my meagre supply of cash: I suppose I should have had more. I casually asked an interpreter of some sorts where I could exchange my Finnish money for the local currency. To my horror, my 39 Finnish marks were valued at just 1 rouble and 90 kopeks by the 'finance minister' sitting in a corner of the hall. Was he a real money changer, or just someone doing it for fun? I still don't know today.

After the Customs inspection, I climbed into the carriage with a cheerful old Ingrian woman, whom I ended up talking to. She was only permitted to travel in one of the carriages designated for those from her country. My second-class carriage had already been detached from the train; I didn't have a ticket for the sleeping car.

The train was an experience. Black, dirty and full of noisy passengers. Makhorka[3] fumes parched my throat and made my eyes water. There was this one big man who blew his makhorka smoke quite shamelessly straight into my face and made me choke. But Grandma didn't even notice and went on telling her stories. I don't remember whether the trip took one or two hours before we stopped at Leningrad's Finland Station; I just remember the timidness, fear and uncertainty, which gradually, metre by metre, expelled all else from my mind. I waited anxiously for new developments.

Through the carriage window I glimpsed a tall man as the train pulled in. I assume he saw me, too, because when I got off the train I found myself facing him, with a shorter man alongside him. 'Well, there you are!' I heard him say. How good it was to feel the squeeze of a familiar hand.

I had known the tall, gaunt Aatto long ago, before he left for Russia. He was a working-class boy from Turku, a talented dreamer, but also ready for action when needed. He had travelled in secret back to Finland, where he was apprehended and imprisoned and sent to the Ekenäs prison camp. He ended up in hospital for quite some time, and I used to visit him a lot. Soon after that, he disappeared to Russia, where he worked as a teacher with his young American wife.

The other member of the welcome party was Arvo, a sturdy, roundish, good-natured man. I already knew him as Aatto's companion from the Ekenäs days; he had lived in Russia for many years, perhaps since the rebellion.

---

3   *Nicotiana rustica*, or strong (or Aztec) tobacco.

9 October 1932

All the while I was staring at the chaos of the station around me, scanning in vain for the others who were supposed to be receiving me. I felt the buzz of the big city. I could see the misery and squalor. It dulled my senses and left me feeling just a vague sense of disappointment. But I tried to rally myself and find the encouragement and reassurance I needed. I mean, here I was in this country with all its great potential where, very soon, the common people would be granted a decent standard of living. Of course, setbacks are inevitable; mistakes happen: Rome wasn't built in a day. But I firmly believed in this ideal of the classless state and that it would ultimately prevail. And so here I was again, like so many times before, whipped up into a passion that was almost like a kind of ecstasy. I barely heard a word my companions were saying until I caught Aatto speaking to Arvo: 'You've still got time to buy those tickets. Get the comfy seats, though, for Kaarina.'

'How about we leave it till tomorrow, so she gets some time to look around here?'

'But where on earth are you off to, boys?' I asked.

Aatto explained, 'Look, Kaarina. It's probably best for you if you rest for a while at the travellers' hostel. Arvo has already arranged that side of things – it's simply a case of staying there a short while. Then, after a few formalities are dispensed with, you can be on your way to Moscow to find office work. In any case, you can rest assured that we have done our utmost with your best interests in mind. You won't understand now, but you won't have anything to complain about. Trust me.'

That was a solemn-sounding speech, especially the way Aatto delivered it, with he and Arvo both standing there stiff and formal. It sounded rather as if Aatto had decided to take charge and let me just tag along. All of which I found pretty annoying. Besides, I had no idea at this point what Moscow might have to offer and I was therefore strongly opposed to the idea.

'I'd prefer to be here in Leningrad, thanks, at least for now. Here I can call my boy in the evenings; and besides, I'm closer to him here.'

'Oh Lord, you're expecting to be making calls home in the evening!' Arvo exclaimed, laughing and gesturing.

'No, Kaarina, that's not going to work! No calls like that, or anything else for that matter. Anyway, how would you support yourself? What would you do and where would you live?' Aatto asked in amusement.

I flared up. How would I support myself? By working, of course! After all, there was zero unemployment in the Soviet Union and I had equal status as a woman. I could stay with my aunt until I got my own room. I grew agitated.

The men seemed like they were having fun; they were laughing at me and were keen to prove how silly I was. I hate laughter when it's used as a weapon to prove a point. It undermines you and only serves to make you defensive. It can get me really angry sometimes.

All the same, I listened quietly to what they had to say. They thought I was that special kind of crazy who didn't understand what was in her own best interests. Everything would be ready for me in Moscow, whereas here I would face unknown dangers, being unfamiliar with the language and not knowing my way around. I said no more and the matter remained unresolved. Arvo suggested going to a restaurant. After we'd eaten, we could find a suitable place for me to stay.

'But I've got somewhere already. It's in a place called Vasilyevsky. I even have the address. I just don't understand why my aunt – my grandmother's sister – didn't show up at the station. Maybe we just didn't recognise each other after all these years? Anyway, it would be rude for me to go anywhere else when I have relatives here.'

The boys glanced at each other again. I started to feel embarrassed about constantly arguing with all their suggestions. But it couldn't be helped.

So, before long, we were sitting on a tram heading to Vasilyevsky Island.

Auntie's apartment was in an unpleasant-looking wooden courtyard. There was no one in; with relief on their faces, the men spun

9 October 1932

around to make their exit. But we ran into my aunt and her husband in the courtyard so we all found ourselves climbing up to the apartment together.

Auntie looked like an old witch. I struggled to equate her with the elegant woman I used to know: the woman who had married a Russian officer in Helsinki, where they had had a good life. They were forced to leave Finland in 1918, and took as much as they could with them. But the contrast between then and now left me speechless. Auntie read my expression, pulled me aside and burst into doleful sobbing. Between the sobs, she spoke: 'Kaarina, dear, that's what this is all about. You will fall apart here, too, just like this home. Do you remember those beautiful red chairs? They were so lovely and the velvet was so soft. It's been fourteen years now. Nothing lasts forever.'

It was hard to listen to, and I could offer no comfort. First, during the war years, they had sold possessions to keep themselves from starving, just so they could eat. What still remained was worn out, and they couldn't afford anything new.

I acquired the necessary permission to move in with them, although apparently the Housing Committee had some very strict rules when it came to foreigners. All the same, in all honesty, their apartment made me nauseous. It was a poor excuse for a home. The kitchen was the worst, with some unspeakable smell, stale and heavy, hanging over everything.

But, for the time being, we parted, and Auntie cried and moaned for an age. How could they be content living like this? A sense of despair engulfed me as I recalled the bright Soviet workers' homes depicted in the advertisements we used to see back home.

I was quite hungry by the time we found ourselves in a hotel restaurant: a long, narrow hall full of diners. The food was good, and there was plenty of it, but it was so heavily seasoned that I was gasping for air between mouthfuls. The orchestra was very accomplished and played briskly.

My first day turned out to be a varied one: we went to a couple more cafés, visited some apartments, and spent the later part of the evening in another hotel with a big ballroom. I didn't know any of the members of our party, but they were friendly. They all seemed to be having fun but I couldn't partake in their joy. I just watched it all as if from a distance. By the time we left, it was so late that it was considered wiser for me to spend the night in the apartment of one of the girls from our party.

And yet, lying under my blanket, I felt miserable and alone. I cried with a longing to go back to where I'd come from.

3

10 October 1932

When the following morning greeted me, I awoke completely rested; I felt like another person. Arvo and I walked into town and ended up at Auntie's place again, where a surprise was waiting for me.

Some time ago I had asked a small favour of a young man called Kari. When I was leaving for Russia, I wrote to him asking him to notify my aunt's family of my arrival. Despite that, my aunt and I had managed to miss each other at the station so I hadn't seen her until I got to her courtyard. Kari had visited my aunt the previous night and waited in vain for me until 1 a.m. But he had left a letter for me, in which he expressed a hope to meet me the following evening. Naturally, I intended to be there.

That evening, I dared to venture out from my aunt's apartment alone. My courage had returned and once again I believed I was on the right path. Even with all its drawbacks, Leningrad was magnificent, and I was intoxicated by its splendour. Come what may, I had to push ahead; the disappointments had to be overcome; frustrations had to be suppressed; we had to adapt to the current situation and have faith in the future. Or that's what I was telling myself as I walked through the city on my own. I felt happy to be alive; the life that lay before me was like a blank sheet of paper. Because of my Poju, I had to succeed. I had to create the best opportunities for him.

There were no quiet whispers in my ears. No pre-warnings. Nothing. No sense that I was walking heedlessly towards the worst nightmare of my life. Towards the darkness. Nobody alerted me.

Auntie seemed pleased to receive me in that narrow space she called her hallway. I went inside where Kari had apparently been waiting for me for an hour. Here was a tall, blond, slender man wearing a Red Commander's suit. His dark-brown eyes were smiling. It was a rare and striking combination, the light hair and the dark eyes.

I was startled to hear him talking to me so effortlessly, even addressing me by first name, yet at the same time there was something honest and refreshing about it. Before long, I found myself discussing my family. How intently and sympathetically he would listen, even though he wasn't disclosing much about himself. The evening flew by, and when midnight came I almost longed to depart with him. He held my hand for a long time and said cordially, 'I just started my month vacation here. I would very much like to be your guide if I may. Could it be agreed that I pick you up around midday? We will go somewhere together. I was born and raised here, so I ought to know my way around this place: it's my home town.'

Why not? I gratefully made a promise to be ready.

In my mind I went through everything I knew about him. His parents had come from Finland to St Petersburg at a young age, his father to be a jeweller's apprentice, his mother into service. After Kari, the family grew with a daughter and then another son. In 1918, their father was claimed by smallpox while in the army; their mother passed away, too, some time after that. With his brother and sister, young Kari went to Finland to live with his relatives in Helsinki for several years. His sister married, as, later, did his brother. Kari, though, decided to return to Russia, where he was obliged to attend military school; he rose rapidly to become commander. That's all I had found out.

The next morning Aatto and Arvo turned up. Aatto looked even more nervous than usual, with the calm Arvo playing a more conciliatory role. There would definitely have been a falling-out between us on the subject of going to Moscow had Arvo not tried his hardest as mediator. We finally reached some sort of settlement. I would stay in Leningrad for the time being: about a month. If by that point I hadn't worked out for myself the difference between Leningrad and

10 October 1932

Moscow, it would be all the same as far as they were concerned. They would wash their hands of the situation and that would be that.

The evening saw Kari return. We had already spent the day looking at the city and now we were taking a long tour along the promenades by the River Neva. I was happy just to be able to talk freely about myself: my son, my parents, everything in my life. I kept on talking all night and Kari, kind soul that he was, just kept listening. There aren't many people who really know how to listen and let you open up, but Kari was one.

The days began to pass more quickly. And each one brought a host of new things. I sought out acquaintances in this city of millions. Some were in schools, dotted around, others were working as clerks or other such jobs. There was quite a lot of difference in how they all received me, although, at first, they all gave me the same look of amazement, followed by the same questions: how had I got into the country? Was I a defector? Did I have a passport? Or had someone 'organised' one for me? Before long, their behaviour towards me warmed, and I was not deprived of company.

Soon, Kari became my shadow, spending all his free time with me. Often, we found the days not long enough, so we would pass evenings at the theatre or, more likely, the cinema.

I had decided I would find work before the end of that October, although I wasn't going to commit myself to anything. I ate anywhere, at any time, mostly with my comrades or with Kari. Everyone stressed what an affordable option Moscow was. However, a phone call to Poju would cause nothing but trouble, apparently, if it were even possible. So only by letter was I able to express my longing for him, to enquire about him, and put into words my hope for an opportunity to bring him to me.

I put my passport details into the register at the House of the People's Commissariat for Foreign Affairs and was given my temporary residence permit. The Housing Committee permitted me to live with my aunt, and my passport had to be checked only once a month at the district police station on behalf of the Housing Committee. So for the time being I was anchored in the city of Leningrad.

4

Late October 1932

The month passed quickly by, despite the pain of missing my Poju. The end was drawing near.

Kari and I still spent our days together, but now he often looked depressed and pensive. Our goodbyes were drawn out, and the atmosphere between us could be strangely subdued at times, our conversation not so light-hearted. For my part, I tried hard to steer our amicable relationship away from courtship, from any pointless fooling around. If in the past I'd ever been lively and witty, I was certainly not going to give him that impression now. Quite the opposite. After all, here I was in a country where true camaraderie was the best it could be, where you could be free and honest, whatever the relationship, whether between a man and a woman or between two men. So I steered Kari away from such dangerous waters, even when the slightest hint arose. That must, of course, have made him draw his own conclusions.

That's when the letter from Arvo popped up. With the October festivities around the corner, he would soon be in town, the letter revealed, whereupon he pressed me about Moscow: had I truly understood the advantages of going there? The letter made me feel positive at first, but then it got me thinking.

I had been making enquiries about jobs: what salaries I could expect and so on. What I found out hadn't thrilled me. There were queues down the streets because of the rigorous card system and the scarcity of goods: everyday necessities were hard to come by. This was not a very appealing environment for an unskilled worker. And yet Moscow, with its apparently ideal conditions, failed to attract me. On the contrary: it scared me.

One evening, Kari and I were strolling casually towards Vasilyevsky Island. We had spent the evening at the great Mariinsky Theatre watching the Soviet ballet *The Red Poppy*. Even though we usually scrutinised everything at great length, we weren't even chatting about the evening's entertainment. Instead, lost in our own thoughts, we passed one corner then another in silence. When we got to my aunt's apartment, I tried to brighten up and offer my usual goodbyes before I ran inside.

'Kaarina, don't go to Moscow,' said Kari.

'So what has suddenly made you change your mind? You've been advocating Moscow more than anyone.'

'Yes I know. And I still can't deny that you'll do well there, but ... I'll miss you.'

These last words came as a low whisper. He pulled me closer.

We stood in silence for a long time, thoughts circling in our minds, orbiting in the same path. In the cold October moonlight everything was hazy blue. Gently, I detached myself from his arms. I said goodbye and crept up to the apartment.

The following day, Kari took up the matter again. Barely was I out of my aunt's earshot before he burst out: 'It just won't work if you leave. Stay here instead: it will all work itself out. We are so different, but I think it would actually be good for both of us.'

For a whole week after that we kept going over it. Kari constantly pressed his point, my own heart was starting to yield – and the time to make a decision was running out.

Kari had a tiny room on the St Petersburg side near the main street of Kamennoostrovsky, although he had to share it for the time being with another Finnish commander. It was almost impossible to get your own rooms in Leningrad unless you had contacts to help you out. Red Commander Vierto was a cheerful room-mate, though, and Kari liked him a lot. You'd be hard-pressed to find a more joyful soldier: he was completely immune to life's sorrows. He was enthusiastically in favour of Kari's proposition and he let his views be known: 'That would almost be a betrayal of the Revolution, Kaarina, if you leave this poor man here behind to pine. Moscow will take care of itself just fine without you, but this place requires the gentle, nurturing touch of a woman.'

All you could do was laugh, really.

★ ★ ★

On 6 November, it was chilly and cloudy with a promise of sleet or snow. But I didn't notice it. My emotions were colouring everything rose, as if it were my wedding day again. But how different was this compared to that special day? No veil, no priest, no guests, none of the trappings of a normal wedding: just the two of us.

After a long search, we found the Soviet Registry Department of Leningrad at the end of a courtyard. What an experience. The waiting room outside the 'inner sanctum' was enough on its own to kill my wedding mood. Every available surface from top to bottom was plastered with advice for young couples. From the devastating consequences of alcohol to the perils of STDs. Charts, graphs, statistics. I just stared at my shoes to try to avoid this horrific bombardment of negativity. Even Kari had to admit that there was too much 'advice' for young couples here and that all those posters were hardly necessary.

The registration itself was quick and easy. My passport, Kari's military statement (only military personnel could legally be in the Soviet Union without a passport), names, professions, ages and addresses. Signatures in a few places and the young pair was ready to step out as a legally married couple.

If you wanted, it could be even more straightforward to get married in Russia. Simply provide the Housing Committee with your own and your spouse's personal information and former addresses. Either form is equally acceptable. If preferred, the registration confers a new surname on the woman, although this is not at all mandatory.

It was the eve of the great Soviet celebration: October Revolution Day, all written in capital letters. Apart from May Day celebrations, this is the only time for festivity in the Soviet Union that goes on over several days. For weeks leading up to the event, the city had been decorated with red flags and slogans, with red costumes much in evidence. To my unaccustomed eyes, it had a market-day feel.

In the evening the city looked so beautiful. The bridges across the River Neva were pressed into service, too, bedecked with strings of lights and calling to mind the stories of *One Thousand and One Nights*. Vessels large and small sparkled on the water, buildings glowed, and the whole sky was ablaze with floodlights. The massive numbers up in the starry sky proclaimed '15': the number of years that had elapsed since Soviet control began. Flags waved, loudspeakers reverberated with music, people surged endlessly back and forth. In the afternoon, Nature made her own contribution by showering pure white snow over all the grey misery.

Kari and I were happy enough with our own party and our own company, soon drifting down through side streets and park footpaths. So many wonderful visions finding form in words: promises just waiting to be fulfilled! Even Poju's future now seemed settled. Soon I would be able to bring him here. We would get him a good education. It wasn't just his own little mother waiting for him now but a good father, too.

But our apartment was just so ridiculously small; the whole floor measured barely 8m^2 and there were already three adults living there. When the few pieces of furniture were accounted for, there was hardly enough room in the middle to spin round. But that would be sorted out long before Poju arrived. Commanders had priority over civilians; and, however hard it might be, I trusted Kari to try his best to get us our own apartment.

5

November 1932

Thus began the happiest time of my life. It was such a short period, but maybe that's why it felt so complete. I tried with all my might to adapt to my new conditions. I closed my eyes and plugged my ears to stop everything that might penetrate and disturb my world of joy. There was a lot to keep out. I tried to forget about all the countless things that I had taken for granted over the years and had thought of as necessities. I forced myself to remain steadfast in my faith in the great project of the common happiness of the people, and the single path by which it could be achieved. I tried to understand everything, to digest it and swallow it. In good faith I searched for just the tiniest sign of things moving forward, for the better. If I thought I might have found one, that brought me joy and kept me looking for more. Disadvantages and deprivations were just growing pains. In any other circumstances, all of this would have quite overwhelmed me – but, as they say, love conquers all!

Time passed and life went on. Kari's job as a Red Troop Commander meant he had to diligently turn up for duty: I was only allowed to have him on his rest days and a few weekday evenings. I escorted him to his barracks, about an hour away, in the morning and in the evening. Just as I was there ready to meet him whenever he knew in advance that he would be allowed to go home.

On his rest days we would set off early to explore the city's shops, market halls and squares. We occasionally stopped at a cafe for a hot drink of some kind and to treat ourselves to some delicious pastries. We would either spend our evenings at home or go to the cinema. The films were brilliantly done, and to begin with they wowed me, Kari's voice in my ear rapidly translating the text. But these propaganda lectures kept coming round again, and they soon lost their power and their appeal. Cinema waiting rooms went to a lot of effort: terrific orchestras to entertain the audience, newspapers and magazines on the tables, along with board games like draughts and chess. The restaurants served whatever they could get hold of. The walls, of course, were covered with propaganda posters.

A circle of acquaintances formed around us. I was lively, sociable and as hospitable as possible considering the circumstances. Before long, our room was often full of young guards who had found themselves in Russia via one route or another, mainly from Finland. There were young commanders, girls and boys, some a bit older, even some comrades born in this country.

Vierto couldn't get a new apartment no matter how he tried, so we were willing to share our little room. He coloured our lives like the April wind: a real rascal – a hero, according to the ladies – and a singing merrymaker with a heart of pure gold. We sang long and often, which must have made the upstairs neighbours think the Finns a musical people. Vierto and Kari would also sing beautiful Russian and Ukrainian folk songs. I could never get enough of those.

6

February to Summer 1933

Three months went by and I found myself pregnant. That really wasn't what I wanted – not yet. No, I was supposed to get some work first, or attend school. What this was all going to mean, we didn't really discuss properly: we just kept avoiding the whole issue from one day to the next.

One day, we visited the editorial offices of Vapaus,[4] a newspaper that was a voice for the Finns. The boss there agreed to meet us, telling me: 'As soon as a proofreading position opens up, you can join our team. It's a good environment to learn the newspaper business. You'd be able to study at the same time. But I'm afraid there's no opening at the moment. Anyway, being the wife of a commander, you're not in any rush to get a job, are you?'

So we decided to wait. And, yes, now there was going to be a baby, and that would disrupt all our plans. I complained to Kari: 'Anyway, how can I bring a little one into the world when there's nothing in the shops to make clothes to swaddle him in?'

A dark cloud descended across Kari's face. I had spoken foolishly.

Quietly, yet deliberately, he said: 'If we can't raise one little one, how do you think the big families are going to manage?'

---

4   A Finnish word meaning 'freedom'.

Under the Sickle and the Sledgehammer

I blushed, my lesson learnt, gently delivered though it was. But in my mind I was already wandering around Stockmann's[5] baby department – oh, how I longed for those lovely, cute, soft things they sold there, which I used to swoon over with my friend. Why shouldn't a Soviet citizen have nice things like that as he embarks on his life? I was already silently rebelling.

And so the little life continued to grow inside me. Expecting a baby and feeling loved: what more in the world can a woman ask for? The expectation of a new arrival softens a man's nature as well – more than you might think. It's partly the miracle of life and partly the ritual of anticipation.

Kari's stock rose even more, at least as far as I was concerned. He looked after me, advised me what was best for me – and even became anxious on my behalf. As for me? I was enjoying life to the full, purring like a pussycat, for once. What else was I going to do?

This whole time I had been keeping in contact with Poju through my mother. I knew all about his health and about his schooling, which he had just started. I knew my Poju was in the best hands, but that didn't stop me from longing for him. I just kept hoping that an opportunity would be round the corner for him to come to me. This sadness – which I didn't wish to bother Kari with – was somewhat alleviated by my pregnancy. So far, it has been for the best for Poju to stay with my parents. We will be together, I told myself, as I stared at a photo of him.

★ ★ ★

In early spring, I was introduced by a military student to Oili Warén – someone I had seen occasionally in Helsinki. She was rather striking and dark-eyed, the wife of a border commander. It didn't take long for us to form a solid bond of friendship, which would come to mean so much to me. Oili's husband was a tall man of few words who had moved from Finland in 1918. They had

---

5 A large, well-known department store in Helsinki city centre.

been married for about three years, and their lively little 1-year-old daughter Aija was their only child together. Oili had a son of about 15, Eero, from a previous marriage, and I have to say it's not often you see such a warm and friendly relationship between son and stepfather. It was readily apparent. Those two comrades could really wind Oili up, yet they always owned up and made amends. Eero was an apprentice machinist in some factory or other, and was bursting with enthusiasm on account of the profession he was working towards.

Oili and I reminisced for hours on end about distant friends in Finland, past events, familiar places. I was shocked to hear her express her downright disgust about what it had been like here since they arrived. My hair would stand on end when she declaimed the uncomfortable truths that I wouldn't have dared utter even at gunpoint. She would say: 'You were a real idiot, Kaarina, to come here for no reason, leaving a perfectly good home – just for this! And don't bother trying to tell me you're happy here. You can deceive yourself but you're not fooling me!'

That's how she talked, even in front of Kari. He would frown but say nothing; after all, her husband was a high-ranking border commander, and educating one's wife falls within a husband's duties.

Spring approached with giant steps. Kari's summer was all mapped out. It would be mostly spent at a military training camp – the summer camps were located in rural villages around Leningrad – with only a few brief breaks back in the city. I was a complete mystery even to myself! I was indifferent to everything, overwhelmed by the happiness inside me. Everything outside my bubble was of no interest. I simply arranged my life and my wardrobe so as to feel as comfortable as possible. Kari and the rest could deal with everything else however they wanted – I didn't really care.

May Day came along with all the big celebrations. Once again, the long rows of flags flapped in the breeze and the red emblems hovered above the streets. The Housing Committee ordered the public corridors, kitchens and courtyards to be tidied up; as for the private areas, it was up to the occupants how clean they were.

Vierto took me to see the parade on the first day. We bagged a great vantage point near the Neva close to the Troitsk Bridge. We stood there for over two hours watching the Red Army march by. It looked tremendous. The wide variety of ordnance – which I, commander's wife as I was, didn't know the first thing about – seemed to be of most interest to the spectators.

A tired Kari only came home later that afternoon. He had been up at 3 a.m. to make his way to the barracks. After an early breakfast at around 5 a.m., they had marched to the parade ground on Uritsk Square. Hour after hour, they were required to keep still, standing to attention and forming lines in anticipation of the march past the tribunal building.

On the second day we went to a party at Kari's unit. The clubhouse was decorated throughout: lots of red. The programme of entertainment in the main hall was varied and it must have been entertaining because, even though I didn't understand the language, I watched it intently.

An enjoyable three-course dinner with pastries was served in the dining room. There were dancing, games and singing in the adjoining rooms. The men were almost all in their military uniforms, whereas the women presented a very varied picture. Brashness and tastelessness were the order of the day: very few outfits that you could call subtle, and, most comical of all, the all-too-obvious creases all over the dresses told a story of being thrown on without going anywhere near an iron. In Finland, it would be unheard of for anyone to be seen even at the most insignificant dance in a creased outfit like that, let alone at a May Day party for military dignitaries. But no one here seemed to care.

Often, when he came home, Kari seemed depressed for no obvious reason. But one mid-May evening, he burst in full of cheerfulness and energy.

'My silly little darling, we have just got very lucky. We can go to Crimea for a holiday for a whole month!'

I could never have expected anything like this: this was really something! I happily started making preparations, as we were to leave soon.

Although this free trip had been granted just to Kari, he had decided to take me with him. The trip turned out to be quite wonderful.

We stopped off in Moscow for twelve hours, so we looked up a Russian family Kari knew and spent most of the day with them. (The train didn't stop anywhere else for any length of time.) We went to the Moscow Red Army House to eat and to visit the museum – about which I can only remember some large paintings of battles.

On arrival in Sevastopol, we boarded a ship which took us to our destination in the Sudak military holiday village. The retreat was a huge place, accommodating almost a thousand guests, plus staff. The buildings were clustered together quite randomly, with a restaurant in the middle where meals were served in two sittings, as not everyone could be fed at the same time. There were crowds of people everywhere: on the beach, in the chalets, in the beautiful rose garden, on the roads and in the mountains.

First, we had to be checked by a doctor, and we were weighed and measured. No special treatments required. After the check-up, we went to find our dormitories, which were in two separate locations: Kari had a place reserved in the men's dormitory, whereas I was in the women's.

The large sports field was permanently crowded, with both women and men playing ball games. Your time at the beach was strictly regulated. The filing system allowed the doctors to sort first-time residents from the rest and allocate them different locations, from where, after a precise period, you were required to move to the next location. If you went farther away, you could lie in the hot sand until you blistered. The children were kept in their own special area, and could leave to visit their parents only at specified times.

It didn't look like there were any other Finns. There was one Finnish commander, though, but he only stayed for a day or two and then travelled back to the lakes of Karelia to do some fishing and rowing. Lounging around in a retreat wasn't for him.

I enjoyed it all. We went for long walks in the surrounding countryside, we swam, and we generally enjoyed our stay. I burnt myself quite badly at first: I was blistered and puffy and I looked terrible. But it soon calmed down and turned into a beautiful tan.

But the holiday came to an end and we found ourselves on the return trip to Leningrad. The train stopped for the entire day in Moscow, so we sought out Kari's acquaintances again and explored the city.

A long, narrow queue for Lenin's Mausoleum snaked around Red Square. Kari spoke to the commander standing by the door, showed him our ticket and explained that our train was leaving soon. So we skipped the queue and went straight in.

Lenin's Mausoleum, a flat building with a flat roof, is on the Kremlin side of the square. On occasions like this, the Soviet government, guests for the festivities and representatives of foreign powers take their places on the roof to watch the Red Army march-pasts. In the shadow of the Kremlin walls is a straight line of thin spruces alongside the Mausoleum. The wall behind the trees has alcoves containing the funerary urns of old Bolsheviks, each with its own plaque.

People file into the mausoleum at a slow and devout pace, welcomed by quiet, sombre music. Lenin lies at rest in a military outfit, badges of merit on his chest. He seems to be just sleeping under the big glass dome. Red Army soldiers stand guard at his head and by his sides, which adds to the solemnity. The room is kept dimly lit – what light there is carefully directed only at the deceased, to draw the gaze. When the eyes alight on that semi-oriental face, it's hard not to ponder whether would Russia be in this state if Lenin were still alive. I have often heard this same thought expressed by many different people. After leaving the Mausoleum, it's a long time before your eyes readjust to the bright sunlight; but the powerful funereal atmosphere persists much longer. It's hard to break out of it.

7

Summer to Autumn 1933

The following day we were back in our little nest once again. Our trip to Crimea – a happiness only granted to the few – was just a pleasant memory.

Kari's unit moved to Krasnoye Selo, and I was left in the city by myself again. Kari took every available opportunity to visit me, even if it was only for half an hour.

I didn't feel bored, though, for I had my own little 'companion', who was increasingly making his existence known to me. I took care of myself with a disciplined routine: I walked exactly the recommended hours and took my rest at precisely the same time every day. Kari always brought his entire ration of food home with him – civilians couldn't really get much in the shops in those days.

I felt content while I waited for my miracle to happen. I can't say the same about Kari. One day, with no warning or explanation, he was transferred by Daily Order and was now the regiment's *fystruk* – sports instructor. Kari complained. Had he been an athlete, the transfer might have been understandable, but this was just another example of the Red Army's insanity – where the stroke of a pen reassigns a man to a position he has no desire or aptitude for. In Kari's case, though, it didn't cause too much trouble and it didn't require him to undertake any further studies. A role like this one is a side job for a Finn in the

Red Army; after all, you only have to be capable of organising. What annoyed Kari the most was that the transfer was like 'being kicked out of the squad'.

'What the hell do they have against me?' he cursed.

'What if it's because you have a foreign wife?' I said with a knot in my stomach.

Kari shook his head sternly: 'I don't think so. Besides, they know that you have already applied for citizenship. What can we do about it if they won't speed things up?'

That was true. I had submitted my application. I had done it with Kari's best interests specifically in mind.

I had submitted all the required information about myself and my family, and I had even signed a small piece of yellow paper – something that I won't be able to forget for as long as I live. It demanded that I shall never, under any circumstances, seek Finnish legal protection, no matter what happened to me. Many times since, that yellow slip has appeared to me in my mind's eye. All the same, even if I hadn't signed it, seeking legal assistance from the Finnish state would never have helped me in a country like the Soviet Union. That is certain. Had I refused to sign, I would have simply put myself forward as a candidate for the list of deportees to Siberia. That, too, is almost certain.

On 11 September 1933 I received an invitation to the Leningrad branch of the People's Commissariat for Foreign Affairs. There I unceremoniously received an officially certified extract from the minutes of the Leningrad council meeting, which contained confirmation that I had been accepted as a Soviet citizen. I was able to apply for a national passport from the militia of my city district.

Once again I had to run to the photographer. Any kind of passport or permit in the Soviet Union requires an impossible number of photos. I had to hand over at least a dozen before I finally got my passport. God only knows where all those photos are now.

8

October 1933

Late on the night of 3 October, Kari took me to the big maternity ward in St Petersburg. Compared to me, he had all the appearance of a beaten dog – men sometimes bear the mark of guilt a little excessively. Once at the hospital, Kari had to wait until all my clothes were catalogued – every single item – and handed over to him. I remained in the facility as naked as my newborn child would be. After an initial check-up of some sort, I saw a nurse approach me with an open razorblade in her hand. I closed my eyes as soon as I saw the worn-out surgical instrument. Just in case, I had brought a Finnish–Russian and a Russian–Finnish dictionary, and in my confusion I almost took them into the shower with me. The nurse hurried over to help.

What I most clearly remember of the maternity ward itself is its terrible coldness. The high iron bed with its waxed fabric cover was like ice. I still remember feeling like I was in a zoo where all the animals are distressed and screaming. There was howling, banging and general noise everywhere. The young nurse and the duty doctor thumbed through my dictionaries with amusement. I shivered from the cold. I was given a thin blanket but it didn't help much.

In the small hours of the morning my daughter was born. The nurse wanted to tell me the baby's gender and tried to grasp the Finnish word she had just learnt, but the doctor beat her to it.

'*Dough* …,' he said.

The sister interrupted and tried to assure me that it was 'all broken'.[6]

For heaven's sake, is my daughter broken in some way?! However, she seemed perfectly intact as they took her away.

As I lay there in the facility, I had time to make comparisons between this doctor and Dr Länsimäki at the Freese Street hospital, where my Poju was delivered. As always happens in Finland, there was a nurse close by to guarantee the patient's safety and to provide assistance. You were reassured by the sight, close at hand, of a meticulous, impeccably dressed nurse – even the beautiful white rosette on her headdress would appear to be smiling at you. But here in this facility all you had were a couple of old, scruffy-looking *njanjas*[7] in their 60s. They were cleaners of some sort who were there to pitch in where required. They were shuffling about all over the place – cleaning the rooms, making the beds, taking patients in and out, handing out food: all of these activities were in their elderly hands. Their shifts were arranged in such an odd way that you might see them day in and day out for a couple of days and then not see them at all for a while. The actual nurses only concerned themselves with administering medication, taking temperatures and giving specialised care. Otherwise, they would pop into the rooms briefly to cast a quick glance while looking impossibly important and distant.

I stayed in the hospital for twelve days so getting home again felt like a celebration. My sweet Pirjo immediately won her father over. To Kari it was almost miraculous that this little bundle was partly his achievement.

---

6   The nurse mispronounced the word for 'boy' by mistake and came out with a word that sounded like the one for 'broken'.
7   Not a qualified nurse but a less educated, older assistant. A Russian word for a childminder or helper.

9

Summer 1933 to Christmas 1933

As soon as we got back from Crimea in the summer, I went to see Oili Warén. By then Oili had already received a massive blow. In mid-June, her husband Urho had been arrested on a tobacco-purchasing trip. Oili hadn't heard about it until the next day during home inspection. And so began her hopeless wanderings from one prison gate to another – there were so many of them in Leningrad. But everywhere she went asking for Urho, she was met with the same cold reply: not here.

At the time of his arrest, Urho had all the family's food cards and money in his pocket, which were never seen again. Around the same time, Oili got into a dispute with the Housing Committee about taking in a lodger. No wonder my friend was so nervous and chose to spend some time in the Kondopoga countryside visiting her brothers.

Over the spring and summer of that year, several Finnish commanders were imprisoned in Petrozavodsk and Leningrad. These imprisonments are generally referred to as the 'Year of '33 Purge'. No one could say why they happened; rumours and assumptions abounded.

In November, Oili came back from Kondopoga with her daughter and dropped in to see me.

'Are you aware, Kaarina, that the Urpola boys, Alpo and Uuno, as well as Vartia, their uncle-by-marriage, have all been shot?'

'What do you mean, "shot"? Sentenced in court?' I stuttered in horror.

'Yes. Because Toini is a member of the party she got to see the decision. Alpo's wife has been deported to the Caucasus; their poor little disabled child was left with Alpo's sister. How is a distressed mother with lung disease supposed to cope with deportation and separation from her husband and child?' Oili sighed quietly.

It was awful to listen to. I was in shock; even Kari couldn't calm me down, at least not completely.

As for us, life continued unbroken and beautiful. I looked after our little one, and because of her I didn't contemplate going to work. Kari continued to work long, full days. There was something about his deep affection for his daughter that I can't call to mind without tears starting to flow. When he came home late in the evening, he would carefully lift the small bundle into his arms and would go on eating and talking still nursing her in his arms. I didn't attempt to prevent it, even though it would probably not have met Professor Ylppö's standards of childcare.[8] If the child was awake, Kari liked nothing better than to babble at her, while she just stared at him with incomprehension. The central heating didn't work very well first thing in the morning: our room was so cold and it was upsetting to have to swaddle the baby in freezing clothes. Kari always woke up at feeding times, and put nappies and rags under his nightgown against his bare skin to keep them warm until I had finished feeding. It felt like he was desperate to spend every possible moment with her, as if he knew that the time would be cut short.

The day before Christmas Eve, Kari left for the barracks just as he always did. Half-dressed, I said goodbye to him, shivering at the door in my nightgown.

'Are you coming home earlier tonight?' I asked.

'I can't say. If I'm not here by about 7 ...'

'... then you'll be here later,' I laughed, finishing his sentence.

---

8   Arvo Ylppö was a famous Finnish professor of paediatrics.

Another wave of a hand by the stairs, a smile and a gentle gaze – and just like that he was gone. Gone – yes, gone for a lifetime. Away from our little 2-month-old baby.

It was the last time my eyes saw him and my ears heard him: a man for whom my heart has never stopped beating. That unsuspected moment of farewell is forever engraved on my mind. It still seizes me even now, after all these years, at the very core of my heart.

As I went back indoors, I had no idea I had just taken leave of my husband for the very last time. I jumped into the warm bed, pulled my girl up next to me and fell back into a blissful sleep.

Kari did not come home by 7 p.m. But that was such a common occurrence, so there was no need for concern. I waited until 11 p.m., as I had done before, the table laid and the food in the oven. Then I went to bed with no idea what was to come.

10

Christmas Eve 1933

At 3 a.m. there was a loud knock on the door. I turned the light on and opened the door. There stood the matron of our apartment (a grandma named Hovila, who lived next door to us and whom I called 'Auntie'), a tall diamond-collared commander, a member of the Red Army with a bayonet, and a member of the Housing Committee, a caretaker of some sort. I was quite astonished.

The horrified old matron hastily explained, 'I just don't understand it: they want to inspect everybody.'

So it's a home inspection then! What does this actually mean? Oh my God! I panicked and then realised I needed to put some clothes on. The commander went to work without asking. He checked everything in our little room. Some of my photos, all of my correspondence, my songbook, my diary, Kari's military documents, his papers, his binoculars and so on – all of them confiscated. Finally, I was made to sign something to acknowledge the items being seized and to waive my right to complain about the home inspection. Whatever would I have to complain about? I felt numb and my heart was pounding out of my chest. So they had put Kari in jail – but why? Why? My thoughts ran round in chaotic circles over and over again. Everything was tangled up in my mind with intermittent bright flashes interrupting and dazzling me. What was to happen to me and tiny Pirjo now?

When they'd finished with our room, the inspection moved on to the matron's side of our adjoining wall. My girl woke up; I fed her, changed her nappy – all the time I was consumed by an ache and a feeling of anxiety.

After searching the whole apartment, they hung around to wait for their transport. It was a wait that dragged on for hour after hour, all the way to 8.30 a.m. The commander sat on an ottoman next to my bed: there was no room anywhere else. The Red Army soldier dozed off by the open door, leaning on his rifle; the caretaker snored loudly in the hallway.

Time stood still. I twisted and turned; I was afraid of my own thoughts. Eventually, I went into the empty kitchen where I was sure to be away from watchful eyes; only then did the tears start to fall. My crying progressed into a ferocious hysterical wail which echoed through the night. It brought the others into the kitchen: the commander, the caretaker and the matron; only the soldier remained unmoved by a woman's screams of anguish.

My cries subsided as the matron consoled me. I heard the commander say that I had no reason to be nervous: nothing had happened to me. Having said that, he left.

Nothing had happened. Nothing had happened when the GPU (State Political Directorate)[9] took the man I loved, the father of my child, the only person we have here in this foreign country, into custody? Really – nothing had happened!

I regained some composure and made it through the rest of the night. When the car arrived in the morning, the commander and the soldier gathered the items they had seized. The commander said something to the matron, and her face twisted. She also got dressed and with a trembling voice said to me, 'He's ordered me to go with him. I don't know what it's about.'

'Oh, Auntie, don't be long. I'm afraid to be on my own,' I pleaded.

---

9   The early Soviet political police agency, a forerunner of the KGB.

Christmas Eve 1933

So I was left alone in the middle of a ransacked room. No matter how much I wanted to throw myself on my bed and cry, just cry, I couldn't. No more tears left.

Just to do something, I set to work. As if compelled by an inner rage, I undertook a complete, major clean-up operation: took all the bedclothes out, washed and dusted – with such speed you'd think the house was on fire. I continued for a few hours until the living room and kitchen were all in order again and I was dead tired. Work: what a blessed help. What a relief it can be in times of sorrow!

The matron wasn't coming back. While I was waiting for her, I got a dictionary out to tackle the copy of the minutes that the commander had given me. I finally worked out that the matron had been arrested too. So I was all alone.

It is futile to try to convey in words the loneliness I felt that day, the torment of the night, and the pain of contemplating the times ahead. A heavy, solid grief engulfed my whole being.

In the evening it dawned on me that in Finland, where Christmas Eve was celebrated, they would be lighting the Christmas tree candles. In my mind's eye I saw my son's radiant eyes, my smiling mother and my father beaming with satisfaction. Yes, of course they had no idea that I was sitting in the dark, so alone, so isolated, a suppressed pain in my chest, little Pirjo in my arms. It didn't feel like Christmas to me.

But life had to go on. The child required dedicated care. As time passed, hope grew. Kari was innocent, wasn't he? He would come back. I just had to endure, to endure.

A few days later, Vierto came by: he had finally moved into his barracks. He found me pacing the room from one end to the other, having lost a lot of weight, a child in my arms. The news of Kari's arrest was a complete surprise to him – a blow.

'Don't talk rubbish, Kaarina,' he said. He was angry at first but eventually believed me. He took control of the situation: first he comforted me and then he considered the financial implications.

'Don't go worrying for no reason: Kari will be back. It's just a mistake that will get cleared up in due course.' He took the girl in his arms and said with a tenderness that I'd not seen in Vierto before: 'Until then, I will act as Pirjo's guardian, and you can't go without food either, Kaarina. After all, you put me up here for so long.'

He kept his word. He brought his entire military food ration for me while he ate in the expensive commanders' canteen; he came to see us every day; he carried the wood inside and chopped it; and he helped in many other ways.

Other friends came to see me, too. Oili visited, her heart full of condolences, even with her own grief to contend with. Aune Lahti from Petrozavodsk was studying to become a teacher, and she stayed with me during her winter holidays. She hadn't dared tell me the story of her companion, but I heard it from others later. This companion was a young woman also studying to become a teacher: she arrived in Leningrad to try to find out something about her imprisoned husband, Commander Salonen. 'Shot back in the autumn' was the short response the young wife was given.

I went to the headquarters of Kari's unit. For an interpreter, I had managed to find a Finn from Petrozavodsk, Commander Mäki – a big, blond man, calm in his manner and his speech, and an excellent interpreter. The commander in charge of the non-commissioned officer training school was a former tsarist officer, a short and stocky man. He received us kindly as we found ourselves in the company of him and the chief of staff. Having heard our case, both officers left. On their return, the chief of staff smiled and explained that my husband was supposedly on a 'secret mission'. I had no reason to worry, as I would still receive the money, the food and the firewood from the army. At least that seemed positive. But a secret posting – rubbish! Families of men on secret missions didn't receive home inspections – that much is certain. My husband was sitting alone in a cell in Voinova Prison, I was sure of that.

Anyway, once again I was in receipt of the plentiful food ration – a benefit that was inaccessible to the civilians queuing outside empty shops. The monthly ration of an officer in the technical unit was: 18kg of bread, 8kg of wheat flour, 900g of butter, a litre of cooking oil or 1kg of fat, 4.5kg of groats, 5kg of meat, chicken or other poultry, 2.5kg of fish, 250g of soap, 50g of tea, 3kg of onions, 3kg of carrots, 3kg of beets and 14kg of potatoes. There was some variation, of course: something might be omitted, something else might be replaced, but this was roughly what we got.

At home, a surprise awaited me: a card from Kari – not from any 'secret posting', but indeed from the prison on Voinova Street. He wrote: 'Happy New Year to you and my little one. Kiss her and teach her to say "Dad", even though I'm not with you. Treat her like the apple of my eye, and don't forget that I am constantly waiting for the day when I can come home and hold you both in my arms. If you can, please bring me tobacco, bread and sugar. Your Kari.' That was all in Russian, of course, but Kari, being from St Petersburg, did have an excellent command of Russian.

The card made life a lot brighter: at least now I had some kind of connection. I took a package to Voinova containing clean underwear and socks. But my visit was in vain: the clerk told me coldly, 'Not allowed to receive packages.'

The packages were received according to alphabetical order of prisoners' names on five days of the six-day week; the schedule meant that everyone knew when it was their turn. A queue snaked in front of the hatches. People looked grey and depressed, the fate of their imprisoned loved ones weighing heavily on them. In addition, everyone was conscious of being watched on account of their captive relative.

Behind the hatches, the inspection was annoyingly slow and lazy. The queue barely moved forward.

11

January to May 1934

Oili received a card from Urho. It was an invitation to say goodbye to him. His case was now clear: deportation to Siberia was imminent.

The autobiographies of the revolutionaries have those gruesome passages where they describe their deportation by imperial law to the cold, barren Siberian landscape. So what was so different under the Soviet system? The destination for imperial deportations still served its old purpose well: an ever-increasing flow of unhappy citizens, cheap labour, people fobbed off with very little and exploited for a lot more. At least it used to be possible to find out the reason for the deportation – along with where to and for how long – but now, except in very rare cases, no information was given either to the convicted person or to the relatives. Sometimes, after relentless enquiries, you might learn that such and such a person had breathed their last somewhere on the Siberian plains.

At the same time, in Finland, the left-wing newspapers were sounding the alarm about every single arrest made by the Finnish authorities. Sometimes, even in the midst of my grief, I couldn't help but respond with a dry, hollow laugh to all the things that had happened. Layer after layer of gold veneer had peeled off the much-vaunted Soviet treasure, revealing its true colours. It was impossible not to compare the promise with the reality. I couldn't suppress my thoughts. I still wanted to believe, but I couldn't.

So Oili finally met her Urho. He had lost a lot of weight. Little Aija, to her father's great sorrow, was afraid and refused to sit on the knee of that bearded old man. The guard, accustomed to people saying their farewells, didn't pay them too much attention; the couples were sometimes allowed to exchange a few words in Finnish. Oili never did learn Russian, nor did I. Urho had faced rigorous questions about Kari, but he didn't know enough about Kari to satisfy his interrogators. Urho promised to try his best to appeal against the sentence; if that didn't succeed, he would work over his prescribed hours, which would shorten his deportation period to three years.

Oili cried as she told me all this. She had tried to see her husband again, but when she arrived at the arranged time it was already too late. Urho was on his way to Siberia.

I, too, submitted an application asking for permission to meet Kari. The day of the visit to Voinova Prison came, and I took Pirjo with me. People were standing shoulder to shoulder: rooms, corridors and stairs were all full, everyone crammed together. Weaving through with the child in my arms, I got to the hatch and got my petition back. Written diagonally across it was: 'Not granted'.

I tried to deliver a package to Kari, but five times it was denied before, finally, my petition was approved, and the package was inspected and taken to Kari.

I got two more cards from him: beautiful, loving words. When I got the last card, I asked my Ingrian milk lady to translate it for me, because it was in Russian again. However, we had to go downstairs and ask a Russian couple instead because the old Ingrian lady couldn't read. Vera the Russian read the card aloud in her native language and burst into tears. I was alarmed: what did the card say? The Ingrian lady, still crying, tried to translate it into Finnish for me but she must have got it very wrong. According to her, Kari's card stated that he would never kiss Pirjo's little hands or feet again.

I left the tearful women and took the card back to my apartment. My ears were buzzing, and my legs were shaking. Eventually, I passed out.

Vierto happened to stop by the house around then. He found the doors open, and me, having fainted, at the end of the hallway in front of the kitchen door. By the time I came round, he had carried me to the bed and was standing beside me, looking deeply concerned. I must have hit my head on something because it felt sore. I cried and told Vierto about the card, which had been found next to me in the hallway. He translated it into Finnish for me, and the situation now became a little brighter.

'It just goes like this: "I still can't say when I can caress my sweet Pirjo's little hands and feet – but I will not stop waiting for the day. I kiss you and I ask both of you not to forget Kari."'

That was Kari's last card – although I was now allowed to take him food and clean clothes every week, which were exchanged for dirty ones. That was enough of a connection to nurture my hope of his release. Otherwise, my life fell adequately into place during those months of waiting. I took up sewing and did what I could to make a living.

In late January, I went with the interpreter to Kari's barracks to apply for my husband's military salary, but the chief of staff, who had previously been so polite, was a different man and received us with utter coldness.

'Former Company Commander Ora, Kari Karlovits, has been discharged from the Red Army,' he said. 'Therefore, we are under no obligation to pay either his salary or any other fringe benefits. That's all. Goodbye.'

On eighteen separate occasions I managed to get a package to Kari before they stopped me and the packages didn't get through any more. In my poor attempt at Russian, I asked whether Kari was still there at Voinova or if he'd been moved to another location. I gathered from the response that he was indeed still there. The following day I sped to the GPU information department. I queued for some time before I heard that the interrogations were over but the verdict was yet to come in.

A week later, I tried again with another package, this time with a note written in Russian: 'If my husband is not here, please write and tell me his current address.' The clerk read it and wrote underneath it: 'Come back again with someone to act as your interpreter.'

And it was exactly during this time that Pirjo contracted severe pneumonia. I thought I was going to lose her, too. Even the doctor was worried and wasn't offering much hope. I stayed up night after night caring for my child, and worked feverishly during the day: it was the week leading up to May Day and people were eager to get their outfits ready for the celebrations.

The last two nights were so miserable. I was like a ghost from all the lack of sleep, the fatigue, and the anxiety about losing my only one. Pirjo slept like a corpse, her eyes deep in their sockets. Following the doctor's advice, I expressed the milk from my breasts and poured it on the child's lips with a spoon: she had no strength in herself even to suckle. I didn't cry, but a wordless chaotic prayer – to Someone – rose up within me from my pain: a plea just to spare my loved one.

And, as if by a miracle, her condition improved. Even the doctor was baffled. Gradually, the child recovered. I slept on the floor beside her, hoping to regain my strength. During that period, I couldn't leave my little one, not even for Kari. So it wasn't until the tenth day of May that I went to Voinova with Kari's old aunt, Anna, his maternal uncle's wife.

Aunt Anna deserves her own chapter. It would be a heartbreaking tale about an orphaned Finnish girl from Ingria, about old St Petersburg and domestic service, about a man, and about their little ray of sunshine who departed this earth in her third year, about the chaotic years of the Civil War, a husband's disappearance, the hopeless waiting, year on year, enquiries that led nowhere. It would be a story of suffering that chills the heart, tears at the nerves, and ultimately numbs you from the inside out. And that would be Aunt Anna's life story.

We took the convalescent Pirjo with us. The ward manager at the hatch urged me to wait with the child on the street, while he escorted Aunt Anna to the Voinova Prison governor's private room.

I waited expectantly with a tortured mind. Finally, Aunt Anna appeared at the gate, clearly in shock. She adamantly refused to say a word until we were home. I was forced to go along with what she wanted.

Many times have I relived in my mind what occurred when we got home that day. I can see dear Aunt Anna, her lips clenched, trying to stand tall, ordering me in a trembling voice, 'Sit on the couch!'

'Oh dear Aunt, don't make me wait any longer. Just tell me.'

'I'm not saying anything until you sit down!'

'All right then,' I said and sat down, just to comply.

I could see Aunt mustering all her courage. In the emotion of the situation she spoke in Ingrian dialect, the words forced out from her mouth, almost as if she were angry: 'The High Court demanded Kari's life. And they got it.'

Of course, that was an oblique way of putting it and I didn't immediately get it, so I demanded, nervously, 'Just tell me straight: this is driving me crazy.'

'Well, the thing is ... they've got rid of Kari. They've shot him. Do you understand now? Shot him!'

Well, that ... that was plain and simple. It hit me like a fearsome blow, not fatal but delivering so much pain.

I remember getting up robotically, as if I subconsciously had somewhere to go. I stood in front of the mirror, lifted my hand up as I had done a thousand times, and arranged my hair without really being aware of what I was doing. Apparently, I remained there for a long time. When I finally moved, I saw Aunt's horrified eyes staring back at me. She told me later that she thought I was about to go crazy.

'Please just say something,' she pleaded quietly.

Suddenly, my head hurt so badly, so the pain must have been real. What was it that Aunt had just said? That Kari is not with us any more? I came to a halt in the middle of the room and shouted in desperation, 'Kari's gone?'

Aunt Anna tried to get me to sit down. She put little Pirjo in my arms and told me to feed her. She told me to cry. But who on earth can cry on demand? I didn't have the strength even to understand what she was telling me to do. Mechanically, I offered my breast to the little girl. Aunt took her away again afterwards, changed her and put her to bed. Quietly, she brewed some tea, set the table, and kept a constant eye on me. Through my neighbours, she sent word to the pharmacy where she worked, and, claiming she was ill, got her predecessor, another old cleaner, to fill in for her. I had no perception of any of these things happening around me. I remained frozen like a statue, no thought in my head other than that Kari was no more. I sat without tears, without a sigh.

Only later that evening did I think of Poju and my mother. I picked up a pen and paper and wrote some cryptic words about Kari being asleep and me being alone ... so alone. Doing that gave me some slight relief: it kind of removed the numbness a little. But it still didn't make the tears flow.

12

Spring 1934

My life became impossible. It was months before I was able to get some proper sleep. In the first few weeks I don't think I slept at all — just some sort of doze that I could fall into from time to time, though it wasn't actual rest. Sometimes I would wake up at night, screaming and shaking, remembering nothing.

But that was not even the worst of the ordeal. It was my own thoughts that terrified me the most. I couldn't shake myself free from thoughts of suicide: they plagued me incessantly like a remorseless headache. I wanted to escape from my life completely and take little Pirjo with me, to where Kari had already gone.

I kept thinking about how we could take our leave as painlessly and quickly as possible. I couldn't escape those thoughts, even though, one by one, I mentally abandoned all the various methods of achieving that goal. My thoughts always went down the same path, both daytime and night-time. I became wary of other people, afraid of everything. I lost weight because I barely ate. My sleepless repose failed to give me any strength; it just drained me even more.

Who can I thank for preventing me from ultimately going crazy? Above all, Aunt Anna, Vierto and Oili. They did everything they could for me. Vierto kept me financially afloat, as I was no longer able to work, Aunt Anna took care of the household, and Oili finally took me to see a doctor, fearing for my sanity.

The doctor was an old grey uncle, definitely a 'former'.[10] During the day he probably worked in some laboratory or hospital; only in the evenings was he free to operate his private practice. There was no separate consultation room; his hallway gave directly onto his only room, which functioned as bedroom, consultation room, dining room and living room. How many things were crammed into that little space! They were probably what was left of the contents of a previous apartment with half a dozen rooms. The walls were filled with paintings, photographs and deer antlers; all kinds of trinkets lay everywhere, in the corner was a modest bed, and across the room was a small glass cabinet containing medical instruments.

The old man was a sweet little goblin, rubbing his hands and beaming warmly. My interpreter explained my condition. The man wanted me to tell him everything. 'Aha, I see, yes!' He listened to my chest, tapped my knees, examined my eyes, and asked about my life.

'From Helsinki? I've been there: beautiful and clean as I recall!'

He said I needed to take this seriously because if I didn't my nerves would fail me. I had to remember that I was a mother, and a bad one at that if I didn't consider my child and show a desire to get well. He prescribed me something to give me some energy as well as some sleeping pills.

Maybe it helped. Gradually, I felt a change coming over me. In time I learnt how to sleep again, and I banished my gloomy thoughts. Because of Pirjo, I tried to get out of the house occasionally and forced myself to eat, whether I wanted to or not.

---

10 There is no clear evidence for what is meant by this. Most likely, he was a former 'tsarist': someone of privileged status before the Revolution, possibly even a lower-level aristocrat. The quantity of possessions in his small room attests to this.

Spring 1934

But the Housing Committee was my next problem. I got a frosty eviction order because I wasn't an owner.[11] By this time, I had already been forced to vacate the room where Kari and I had lived. Apparently, once Kari's verdict came through, I should have just quit the house completely and gone to live on the street, for all they cared. An order like this was nothing new under the Soviet star.

In addition, the People's Court had sent a summons to Kari because he had taken out a loan from the army commanders' loan office. That, of course, could not be repaid from prison. So where would I get such an amount? Someone told me my sewing machine would be taken away if I couldn't pay the loan off.

The Housing Committee harassed me about bringing them Kari's death certificate and the deportation order for my former matron (she had been sentenced to three years' deportation). All else failing, I had to get an interpreter and go to the GPU information office to ask about the necessary documentation. It would really have been catastrophic had the Housing Committee been allowed to throw me onto the street with a 7-month-old baby. Or even if they had the right to take away my main source of income: the sewing machine that had been imported from Finland.

Around the time I first arrived in Leningrad, I had witnessed a small church being demolished. I remember feeling sad for the beautiful building. Now, a year and a half having passed, I walked into a new house built on the exact same site. On the Liteyny Avenue side, there were all sorts of chambers and offices. Using the side-street door, my interpreter and I managed to find the right department. The waiting room was crammed. After a long wait we found ourselves in front of the officer in charge. From behind a card file he told us to be seated.

---

11 Occupiers didn't own their apartment or room but could have a share in the housing co-op (run by the Housing Committee). This conferred a right to live in the building, although one's housing 'need' was dictated by the Housing Committee. A single individual could not expect to occupy a large space. Subletting was permitted only with Housing Committee approval but, equally, a sublessee could be assigned if an occupier was thought to have more space than they needed.

Behind our backs, at a smaller table, sat another officer in military uniform, staring at us, a small handgun on the table just in case a prisoner's family member decided to raise a commotion for some reason. Anyway, we had no such intentions, and neither did anyone else. This solemn ritual felt theatrical and pointless.

The bored-looking first clerk explained that Kari had indeed already received 'the highest judgement' and had been executed.

'And for what reason?'

'According to the letter of the law, Section 56, Paragraph 8.'[12]

'What does that paragraph say?'

'You need to request the information yourselves – from the District Prosecutor's office, for example. We're not required to explain it.'

A weary gesture indicated the door.

And so we left, having forgotten to ask any other questions. This actually turned out to have been all for the best. The next time I was face to face with a clerk, he was much more humane – at least less weary and bored. This clerk explained that certifications of convictions were never given to individuals, so the Housing Committee had to either take my word for it or request confirmation via its own organisation. The People's Court would definitely allow the matter to lapse, as long as I informed them about my husband's verdict. I didn't have to move out; I had the right to purchase a share in instalments so long as I was in employment. If they tried to evict me in spite of everything, I just had to seek the help of the district ombudsman; because of the child I wouldn't be forced to move out, at least not onto the street. Although I was the widow of an executed man, I still had the right to do productive work wherever I could.

Of course, I tried to organise things as best as I could, but they really made me run around for it. The hardest thing was getting an interpreter. It wasn't a very enticing offer, helping the widow of an executed man, even as an interpreter. Caution was required. For

---

12 In reality, the conviction was most likely based on Section 58, Paragraph 6, which deals with espionage and working against the government; this was the section most often referenced when sentencing ethnic minorities.

example, about a year after Kari's execution, someone received severe chastisement at a party meeting at his workplace, just for having been my interpreter. His party membership was revoked and he was later imprisoned. He should not have got involved with the 'enemy', never mind that he was only taking pity on the poor suffering mother of a young child. But I was, God help me, the widow of a traitor, a spy, a class foe.

Wise people avoided my company; when they saw me, they hailed me from a distance, hoping I wouldn't stop and talk to them. It was always better to be careful than to regret it later on.

The Housing Committee gave up and I got to stay with no further disturbance. The People's Court was satisfied with my explanation of Kari's death and demanded no further compensation from me.

Getting a job, on the other hand, seemed hopeless. The director of the Finnish publishing house had already indicated, via an intermediary, that it would be questionable to hire a widow who was 'so close' to the case. I sold Kari's clothes: in Russia second-hand clothes were highly sought after. I did some occasional work at home and got by in a modest way.

Life hardly felt worth living. My only joy was Pirjo, but that was mingled with depression. Why had I not been able to share this girl with Kari, so we could follow her development together and enjoy her? But you have to make do with the cards you have been dealt.

So many times now I inwardly cursed my decision to come here. I had without doubt made the most serious mistake of my life. My only relief was that I hadn't dragged Poju into this misery, but in reality that was only because of my parents. How often I sighed with relief to think about that. At least Poju was having a happy childhood and looking forward to a good future in Finland. But what about little Pirjo's future? Gloomy, grey and hopeless. As the wife of an executed man, my only undisputed right was hard manual labour, from which there would never be an opportunity to rise and see better days. As an outsider, the shackles of my past bound my feet; I was permitted to shuffle along and no more. I knew my past would never be forgotten here. What about Pirjo's future? She was branded, too: she was her father's daughter. Even if she learned to hate her father and curse him, as Soviet doctrine required, she would still be under suspicion, both behind closed doors and in public. Did I still have the strength to make her believe, despite my own suffering, in the good that was supposed to be inherent in this system? This society, with its glittering outward appearance, attracted thousands with its twinkling lights and make-believe promises of happiness; yet before long your eyes were opened to the terrible Moloch endlessly devouring the best and the most beautiful while mercilessly destroying homes, families, people.

I had passed the rigorous first term at Stalin's higher education facility. Being unprepared and sensitive, I found it the hardest. Later I became more seasoned; the punches still hurt, but it was nothing I'd not felt before. There were no more surprises. I was prepared for anything.

13

Summer 1934

Fate decided it was time to turn the next page in the book of my life.

Until now, I had remained steadfastly in the realm of the home and had seen the world through the eyes of a woman in love. I had been conciliatory and acquiescent, when, in any other situation, I would have been horrified and fled.

Now change beckoned. I had to step outside the safe orbit of my home life and fight for my own survival – I had to engage with the world outside. The first step was to get some kind of job, whatever was available.

With Oili's help, I got taken into the 'bristol' factory. That word – 'bristol' – still sounds like gibberish to me. Perhaps I can make it clear by explaining what they actually made at the factory. They created some kind of thin cardboard, mainly those thicker pages you get in books between the actual pages and the cover. Thinner cardboard was also made thicker by being glued together to make the board for book covers. In addition, they made art paper for colour plates, which was decorated and trimmed to size.

I ended up in the drying room, where large furnaces heated the atmosphere to a temperature in which the glued sheets of paper, hung on metal wires across the ceiling, could dry within two hours and then be replaced with the next batch. Meanwhile, the workers were heaving massive stacks of wet, glued paper onto the presses.

The presses were old German-style machines, but the controls were all broken: we had to use iron bars and brute force to operate these aged contraptions – we must have looked like old pictures of medieval slaves. In fact, the work of a dryer was as hard and as sweaty as the work of any slave. We left the oppressive drying room with our clothes soaking wet, and would then be shivering in the cold basement.

The monthly salary started at 115 roubles, and could increase to 148. I was an additional worker (plans were made at the beginning of each year in which the number of employees was determined; food cards were issued based on this number alone) and so I didn't get any food cards – nor did I receive a 'broon'. This was a slip or permit, allowing access to crèches and kindergartens; the workplace purchased them from the state, also at the beginning of each year, for its female workers. The broon holder was given a discount on the childcare institution's fees, and you couldn't get your child in there without one. Of course, being an 'additional' worker, I had to 'hit and run', as the Russian proverb goes, all these different places until someone saw me as a charity case and I was granted permission to keep my child in a crèche during working hours. It took sixteen separate certificates – from various doctors, the Housing Committee, the factory manager, the factory committee and heaven knows where else – before I got my girl inside the building with me and actually got down to work. This *volokita* – a plethora of paperwork and bureaucracy – is prevalent throughout Russia, wherever you go; even the simplest matter can't be resolved without it.

Pirjo was small and frail. Despite all my efforts, I couldn't raise her into the kind of healthy, handsome child that Poju had been. It was sad to have to hand her over to others to take care of, but you do what has to be done. The crèche worked in two shifts, but I had three shifts. So, during the night shift, I had no choice but to leave that tiny child to sleep alone within those four walls and behind a locked door. How could I have paid for a night-time carer on my meagre salary? The Housing Committee had, in the strongest possible terms, threatened me with eviction and refused permission to sublet. There was no choice. I just had to swallow any resentment, pity and fear and keep on working — one night at a time.

I was in a bad way myself. I had to wean Pirjo off around then. Heavy work, long journeys, poor nutrition and a weak body — in those first days of work all of this kept me constantly unwell with a slight but stubborn fever. However, I tried to keep working, despite the humming in my ears and the dizziness. Gradually, the fever subsided and I overcame my illness.

The 'Red Manager' of the factory, as we called him, was one of the Finns from Leningrad; the technical director was Russian. He was a kind-hearted man, the Red Manager, and he did his best to help me, but he couldn't do much. But he did what he could, and often gave me purchase permits. The technical director, on the other hand, treated the workers with contempt, as you might expect from a Soviet leader.

The workers at the factory were mostly Finns or Ingrians: a hard-working bunch who tried their best to give satisfaction, so as to keep themselves out of the firing line. There were plenty of subtle hints, however, among the recollections of times gone by to suggest that this was a forced surrender. You had to be very careful about what you talked about — and whom you talked to.

One day, an old working woman called Alma came up to Oili and me, acting all mysterious, and started telling Oili off for speaking out about this and that — a frequent habit of Oili's, which could be put down to her quick temper.

'But there's someone here listening and taking notes.'

'Pfft. Rubbish!' replied Oili. 'And who cares anyway? So I get to go and see Urho in Siberia. When you're as angry as I am, you can't help speaking your mind.'

Alma, a sweet old soul, leant forward and almost whispered, 'The director asked me a while ago to go and find out what this group is really like. Said it would be easiest for me because you lot always come to my section to eat and chat. My salary would go up as well.'

'Well, well. So what did you think about that?'

'Oh, good lord, Oili, what do take me for? I couldn't do something like that. You say something and the words get changed before they reach the intended destination. Then an innocent person gets taken away and imprisoned.'

'What about the director?'

'He laughed at me – to my horror. Said he didn't realise I was so sensitive. But believe you me, oh yes, someone in here will be taking on that role, that's for sure.'

'Why are you coming and telling us this?' Oili asked.

With an anxious look across her face, Alma spelled it out: 'Well, otherwise you're a nice girl, but you never stop to think about what you're saying. It will get back to you if you don't take more care. Kaarina keeps nice and quiet: she's frightened because her husband's already been shot, but you're so crazy you actually think this is how you can get to see Urho.'

To be honest, I was just as frightened by Oili's loose talk as well. After Alma left, Oili stayed quiet for quite some time. All the same, she didn't really heed Alma's advice: she could still be heard saying something careless every now and again.

14

Autumn 1934

Preparations were under way for the 1934 October celebrations. So I had been in the country for two years and Pirjo had turned 1. The factory was closed down for three days for the party. As a mother of a child under the age of 3, I could not be forced to take part in the celebration march, even though the crèches were open in case the mothers did get involved. Participation in the march was optional, but all the same my name was up there on the 'did not attend' black board after the party. However, the director did remove it seeing as it was there in error.

On the celebration day itself, I had a house guest in the shape of Aarno Kivelä, who had just been promoted to commander. He had been given a month's vacation, but accommodation was a problem. Oili took in Aarno's companion and told me I should put Aarno up. They eventually talked me into it but I agreed only on the condition that Aarno himself get permission from the Housing Committee. The Housing Committee secretary was putty in the hands of the young Red Commander: not a single complaint or objection was raised. My work days were long and I was only in the house for a short while, and so it didn't really matter who stayed in my room while I was out.

Aarno was as pleasant a housemate as you could wish for. I was surprised from the outset that he would even dare to associate with the

Under the Sickle and the Sledgehammer

widow of an executed man, but he also showed me a lot of sympathy. Such open-mindedness made me look at him with a keen interest; indeed, he was a man whom I soon learnt to respect deeply.

I shared my concern with him that it was not a good idea to be staying with me and risk his own future. He said that people preferred not to be associated with me simply out of fear for their own skin, but equally not everyone believed Kari was guilty, even though no one would dare to suggest that a mistake had been made. But because I myself had been allowed to remain free, that was a testament to my own innocence at least. As far as Aarno was concerned, if I hadn't got any problems with him then he didn't care what everyone else thought.

All Aarno's friendly words and kind deeds during that time left me forever grateful and in his debt. I was deeply moved by his courage and compassion. Aarno was a great help financially, too. As well as paying my monthly rent, he brought his magnificent – from a civilian's perspective – commander's food supplies into the house, and had meals waiting for me when I got in from work. He even looked after my little one when needed; I was able to work my night shifts in peace as Pirjo now had a caregiver at home.

The month passed so quickly and, once Aarno had gone, I felt truly alone. Maybe he felt the same: in no time at all, a long letter came in the post. And thus began the correspondence that added some much-needed variety to my lonely life.

The children's nursery was a lot of help for single mothers, allowing them to work, but the crèches could be frustrating. Now and again they might close their doors quite randomly; if a child had been ill, the entire facility was disinfected and closed down for a couple of days. Of course, it was the right thing to do. But where were you supposed to put your child in the meantime? Anyway, I certainly didn't have anywhere else. If I stayed at home, I lost a day's wages. The union didn't assist you unless you'd been a member for at least two years. My monthly salary was nowhere near enough. Crèche fees, rent, firewood, electricity, mandatory tram tickets – the money just dwindled away. And, of course, I needed to eat. After my hard day's work I had to sew to earn some extra income.

Autumn 1934

I sent bright, hopeful letters to Finland. Everything was fine. But what else could I have said? I could have written page after page about how it feels in the morning, at the end of the night shift, trying to board a tram already bursting with passengers and counting yourself lucky just to hang on by your toes and fingertips to the doorway or the bottom step of the carriage. When you find your little darling soaking wet and crying; when you change your baby's wet clothes in a panic, rush her to the crèche before you can finally make yourself a hot drink; when you wake up from a death-like sleep with a gnawing hunger just to grab yourself a piece of pickled cucumber and some black bread, which, because you don't have a food card, you've only been given out of charity. Or how it feels around midnight after an evening shift to be so afraid of the overcrowding on the trams and the delays in case you don't get to the crèche in time – where Pirjo is entirely dependent on the goodwill of the cleaners as the nursery staff have already left an hour earlier; and how it feels to endure the angry looks of the cleaners because I have disturbed their well-deserved night's rest, even though there's nothing else I could have done. I could have explained how it feels to cry with helplessness when, despite constant pleas, food cards can't be issued; how many times I have fainted from hunger; how my weight has dropped to 46kg from somewhere in the mid-60s; and how skinny I am, like an old witch, whose big fearful eyes are the only way you can tell she's still alive.

None of that could possibly have been written, and I wouldn't have written it anyway, even if it had been permitted. I didn't want to upset my loving family; my mother wouldn't have had a moment's peace if she'd been given a glimpse into all the depressing misery in which her only daughter was mired.

For Christmas, a surprise came for me from my mother: a purchase permit for Torgsin, to the value of an amount paid by my mother in Finland. Torgsin was a closed shop where you could buy all the good things you liked: nutritious food, clothes, household goods – just like a Helsinki store. But you could only use foreign currency or take your gold or silver items and exchange them for purchase slips.

I remember when I was living with Kari puzzling about this country's complicated trading system. All the good things were in Torgsin and Insnap. Insnap was the shop that catered to foreign ex-pat clientele: that's where the American Finns got everything they needed in the early years. On a level below that, closed shops had sprung up, which were attached to various institutions and in which there was a lot of variation in quality and availability. Soldiers, militia and GPU officials would all get their substantial food rations from their own particular shops. At the bottom of the pile were the shops for the general public, with their empty shelves, the occasional stock they had quickly snatched up by the crowd.

Thanks to my mother, I was able to buy Pirjo a little woollen garment and some food, and I also purchased a magnificent Christmas present for myself: a coffee tin weighing 150g. How wonderful that tasted to Oili and me – I need say no more.

15

January 1935

A new year began, promising nothing but the same old greyness. Pirjo was ill all winter; when she got over one disease, a new one arrived. But she survived, despite the pitiless conditions.

Aarno's letters were the only moments of brightness in my life. Their tone became increasingly warm, and they repeatedly implied some kind of hope for the future, which left me feeling confused and uncertain.

Hadn't I already had enough of the grey of loneliness, longing for something and not feeling safe as a woman? Had I any objection to Pirjo getting herself a father and living a normal home life, instead of being alone and consistently battered by the world since the day she was born? Did I have any doubts about his paternal qualities? These same ideas were expressed by Aarno, too, in his letters and his poems. He didn't just write to me; he wrote to others as well, sometimes openly and sometimes more covertly, about his intentions towards me. Soon my whole circle of friends was aware of the situation and was following the poet's courtship attempts with amusement. Everyone was insistent that if anyone was a gift from heaven it was Aarno, and he should be welcomed with open arms. They hammered their point home so much that my ears were sore from hearing it. But I couldn't justify the decision to myself that easily.

Oili sometimes got a card from Urho from a large GPU Soviet farm situated somewhere in Siberia's outer reaches. Urho was battling through twelve-hour days to shorten his sentence; he worked as a tractor operator with grit and determination in a job that required a lot of strength and energy. Because of his severe gastritis, he asked Oili to send some dried wheat bread crackers. Obviously, Oili tried to send whatever she could get her hands on.

Oili continued to look after me tirelessly. If she got hold of a decent cut for a stew or to put on the table, she let me know and made me eat. She showed me the kind of affection you'd get from an older sister, and gave me such help and advice that I will never forget her. If I were faltering at work out of sheer fatigue, there she was, right next to me, helping me carry my burden.

In February, Pirjo became infected with whooping cough which she'd picked up at the crèche. A six-week illness is no small matter with no sick pay and no wages. I couldn't help but be anxious. It felt so brutal: never being allowed the chance to make anything work out for me. No matter how hard I tried, sooner or later there was a roadblock ahead and some hardship. It all made me so tired and killed any urge to even try. Perhaps it was wisest, after all, to accept Aarno's offer: become a housewife and fall back into the comfort and safety provided by his broad shoulders. This thought was the spark I needed to eventually come to terms with this course of action.

I told Oili and she was thrilled. She said: 'Look now, Kaarina, the thing is: you won't get anywhere by yearning for the past, however much you miss it. It's all gone, just like Kari. All you get to do now is trudge along with your little girl, treading up and down on the same spot without ever moving forward. I've had to fight for myself all my life, but I still say it's easier with a man when you've got a child to look after. Especially here, where you can't get anything without brute force. Listen, sweet Kaarina, I'm being serious. From the bottom of my heart I hope you marry Aarno – it would be so good for me, too, to know that you are better off.'

I guess she had a point. Oili's good wishes had an effect on how I felt about things.

January 1935

'But just think about it, Oili: because I'm a widow, that could cast a shadow over Aarno's whole future,' I said hesitantly.

'Aarno is a man and is responsible for himself. And I shouldn't imagine the great army would suffer too much if one of its commanders married a slightly suspicious widow,' Oili replied.

Aarno had received a transfer from Inner Russia to join the Finnish troops in Petrozavodsk. It was such a pleasure to read his letters: they were so honest and direct. In fact, he announced, he was currently looking for a room for us, after which he would come and get Pirjo and me. I wrote to him expressing my doubts; in his response he dismissed all the dangers, which made me happy, although my fear of the future was still lurking within me.

16

Spring 1935

Spring approached. I had left the factory and was sewing again from morning until night. Fearing that someone would inform on me to the Housing Committee, I didn't dare ask for much money. I didn't report my work in any way: I just did it in secret, cash in hand. I had heard about the hefty fines some people had to pay. There was a lot of work to be done, and the sewing machine was running all hours of the day.

At the end of March, Aarno got his leave and came to Leningrad to pick us up. However, we stayed in the city for the period of his leave, partly because I needed to finish the work I'd taken on and partly because I found it difficult to leave my friends. It was a pleasant time that I can look back on with no regret.

Aarno wrote a letter to my relatives, no doubt reassuring them about my future happiness. He received a response, which appeared to come as a pleasant surprise. He also received a letter from his comrade-in-command in Aunus,[13] which included some friendly banter about 'settling down'. He read the letter out to me, and, as he was putting it back in his pocket, a strip of something fell out without him noticing it. I picked it up off the floor and couldn't help but read it:

---

13   The Finnish name for Olonets (see map on page 15).

… must seriously warn you against this marriage – it will surely end up being a problem for you. Far from wishing to put pressure on Kaarina in any way – both her and your story elicits all my sympathy and my congratulations – but the party leadership sees only Kari's actions. I'm seriously worried about you. You may end up leading Kaarina and her girl from bad to worse. But this is for your eyes only. Tear it up after you've read it!

Blood rose to my cheeks.

'What is this? Aarno, have you read this?'

Aarno looked up and grabbed hold of the paper. He had started playing with Pirjo and hadn't noticed me reading it.

'Ach, Kaarina, it's all just nonsense: you weren't supposed to see it! Herman has got to be mistaken. And you don't need to worry about it, either; this is my concern.'

He sounded confident and cheery; his assurance was admirable, but I wasn't comforted so easily. I continued: 'All the same, what if we give it up? You could go back and say you came to your senses before it was too late.'

'Don't talk crazy, darling. We are where we are: we are married; and even if Petrozavodsk starts to create trouble, then I will absolutely not change my mind, there is no doubt about that.'

That was the end of that discussion. And next time wasn't any different when I tried to change his mind again. In the end, he wouldn't hear another word about it. I spoke to Oili as well, but her answer was the same: 'Let Aarno take care of the whole thing.'

I told Liisi Urpola about my fears. Her brothers Alpo and Uuno had also been shot. Liisi lived in an apartment with her sister Toini. Toini's husband Vartia had been shot at the same time as their brothers, but Toini was still a party member and a shop steward at her factory. Maybe there had been some error in the GPU papers – but a party member she remained nonetheless, and even continued as one after Liisi was imprisoned and both her ex- and present husbands were deported. So, there had been three death sentences, imprisonments and deportations in the family, but there was the oldest surviving

Spring 1935

sister still carrying a party membership card in her pocket. It was a unique, downright extraordinary situation. Liisi was a blonde, bouncy, happy person. She did a wonderful job of comforting me, exhibiting all her own fearlessness:

'We have all, dear Kaarina, got our names on the GPU papers somewhere; they probably know our shoe sizes, never mind anything else. And it is reasonable to assume, because they haven't imprisoned us yet, that our names are not there in the lists of bad people but we are counted among the decent. Be content and live in peace with your poet.'

But Toini snorted: 'Don't jest. I can understand why Kaarina's afraid. I'm not going to say one thing or another. Whatever comes your way, it will come, whether you are Aarno's wife or Kari's widow. My nerves are always on edge: I don't think it's over for us, either. Who knows what else is coming. I can lose my party membership card any time, but I just want to avoid Siberia because of these children. I don't think I've ever harmed anyone. I was born in this country and I've never been anywhere else — but just all this constant uncertainty.' Toini came to a halt and just made a descriptive gesture, hopeless and tired.

Aarno arranged it so that after the May Day party was over we could go to Petrozavodsk. Dark premonitions followed me there, too.

Later on, Aarno's comrades told me how they had tried their best to talk some sense into him. They had virtually painted a picture of the devil, horns and all, trying to persuade him how bad things were going to be in Petrozavodsk. But Aarno had been unflappable. It wasn't that he had tried to disagree with the boys' warnings: he simply wasn't interested in them; he chose his own reckless path.

On the way to Petrozavodsk, a short and stocky older commander was sitting in the carriage seat opposite. When he got a chance, Aarno whispered to me that he was Akseli Anttila. Anttila was a gifted storyteller, but well aware of his own talent. I didn't really take to him. Maybe he didn't like me either, because he preferred to engage in conversation with Aarno.

'He's probably aware that I'm a widow and he suspects that I'll drag you down with me until we're both outcasts,' I told Aarno, laughing.

'Honestly, you! Anttila is a big chief somewhere in central Russia. He's just on holiday travelling to Petrozavodsk at the moment; why in the world would he care about some new team commander or his little wifey?' said Aarno, and continued telling me what he knew about him.

I had visited Petrozavodsk with Kari in the autumn of 1932. Now, in the spring of 1935, it looked just as grey as it had before, with its small houses and only in the very centre a larger building rising up. I still can't understand why American Finns had allowed themselves to be transferred here to this posting away from the cities.

Aarno had an apartment on the upper floor of a large two-storey log-built house. The house was not owned by the army, but was being leased to the commanders on a temporary basis, until the large stone buildings on Anohin Street had been completed. The eight families upstairs shared a kitchen, and that's where you got to know one another. There were three Finnish commanding families in the house altogether – the rest were Russian – with a couple of Karelian non-commissioned officers on the ground floor.

Back in Leningrad I had already heard from Aarno about my Finnish neighbours. Behind the adjoining wall lived a young commander from Häme province called Lasse Halme with his young wife, Tonja, who came from Kestinge and who wasn't yet 20. The other couple were just as young. Commander Veli Rautio and Lasse Halme had both come from Finland at about the same time, around 1930. Rautio's wife, Norma, was born in America to Finnish parents; she was as lively as quicksilver. They were a little too free, too joyful and noisy for me while I was still nursing my grief. Before long, those high-spirited women didn't feel comfortable anywhere apart from with us; I became like a big sister to them, and a mother besides – someone they had to tell everything to, or ask for advice about the most basic things: 'What meal shall I cook today? Do tell me, Kaarina.' Norma had to be taught how to weave, Tonja how to sew underwear, and both learned thousands of the little tricks of being a housewife.

It was a fun way to pass the time. Pirjo gained weight and built up her strength, finally getting up and walking at the age of 1 year and 8 months. I noticeably regained my strength once I'd had some nutritious food. Above all, Aarno was pleased.

But still our sky was not cloudless. It was more an instinct than anything else. I could no longer really believe in anything good; rather, I was constantly prepared to encounter new blows. I no longer bothered Aarno with my suspicions. Every night I was thankful for the day that had been; I was thankful for the time in which I got to rest and gather my strength.

17

Summer 1935

It was Eino Laine, recently expelled from the army, who brought us the first warning.

'Aarno, I should have told you when I saw you in Leningrad – about Virta's message – but I didn't want to ruin your holiday mood,' he said.

'Well, let's hear it now. The holiday is over,' Aarno laughed.

Eino continued hesitantly: 'Well that's how Virta is – you know what he's like. Though this isn't getting any easier, but you'll hear it from others anyway, sooner or later. Virta is warning you to watch your step. The consequences will be clear if you bring Kari's wife with you to the Petrozavodsk district.'

So that was the message from Virta, the party secretary of the battalion school. But I had enough on my plate with my own issues so I left it there.

Certainly, Eino was speaking the truth as far as his own affairs were concerned! That same spring, he and another commander had been expelled from the army without a word of explanation; the order of the day gave no justification – just dismissed them. Naturally, both of them were currently going around feeling down and very disgruntled. And no one could fathom what was behind it all.

The next day we bumped into a man whom Aarno was familiar with from his time spent in Ekenäs. He was a member of the

Committee of the Regions, and Aarno told him about Virta's admonition. The Committee of the Regions had no knowledge of the matter and, as far as this member's opinion was concerned, it did not need to be brought up and ought not to be. Aarno was capable enough of making his own decisions about whom he married, and there was no reason for anyone else to intervene. I left the men to talk and hurried home on account of Pirjo.

Later, Aarno told me that Virta had turned up in the middle of their conversation, as if on cue.

Aarno had greeted him with irritation: 'Well, here I am in person, so – please – tell me what you think is best for me. Don't you think it's a bit immature to send a message like that second-hand? You should have written to me directly.'

'Yes, and by whose authority do you send your views without consulting other people's opinions? We need every man we can get, especially experienced, seasoned Ekenäs campaigners like Aarno.' Even the Committee of the Regions member was getting involved in the conversation. 'Now is not the time for our forces to fall apart over minor issues.'

Virta was taken aback and strongly insisted that the message Aarno received was just an invention of Laine's own twisted mind; he vehemently denied sending any such message.

'Who knows which one of them is telling the truth; who's got their own agenda?' Aarno mused as he finished recounting the conversation to me.

Some time later, the commanders had been discussing our marriage during one of their tobacco breaks; there had been views for and against. A few more days passed, and Aarno was brought before the commissioner, Comrade Toivola, where he received an earful.

'I don't understand your way of thinking, Commander Kivelä. You know all the aggravating circumstances, you've been warned and advised, but you defy everyone by going ahead with this and bringing the wife of such an undesirable man into the great common family of the Red Army. Do you have no Bolshevik sense of responsibility?

Or did you not even think about your position as commander?' The commissioner's words poured out in one long growl.

'Warned? May I ask, Comrade Toivola, whose warning you are talking about?'

'Comrade Rytty. Didn't he warn you as long ago as autumn and tell you to think about the consequences?'

'That's not true! I've never had any warning from Comrade Rytty. All he did was wonder once how I had come to know Commander Ora's widow.'

'I have a letter from him discussing this very matter. Read it!'

Aarno read the letter. In it, Rytty, a respected high commander in Leningrad, stated that he had warned Aarno to 'not take that step'.

'I don't understand this,' Aarno said. 'Rytty only said to me he wondered who on earth knew to house me at the widower's place. If he thinks he was issuing a warning, so be it. I didn't take it as a warning then, and I don't see it as such now.'

Heated exchanges of words continued into a second hour. Finally, Toivola got up from his desk and barked: 'Well, at least we know now that you are not stupid, but you are someone who has brought a large dose of bourgeois sentimentality with you, along with all that kind of hogwash, despite that fact that you've come from Ekenäs.'

'As a result of this conversation, am I to understand that the party expects my marriage to end immediately?' Aarno asked.

'Good grief, what's wrong with you, man? As a communist, do you think you're improving your cause by making another mistake? Although clearly we oughtn't be surprised if you went and did something else reckless, such as going home and sending your wife packing and out the door.'

Once Aarno had finished relating his conversation with Toivola, the evening was heavy and depressing. Once again, I felt like a persecuted animal. And all because I had loved my husband, the father of my child, in a way I could never again show to another man – not to Aarno, not even now, when he, such a fine man as he was, would be paying such an expensive price. He saw that I was suffering, and comforted me:

'Kaarina, let it be. No one can blame you for this: you are completely innocent. If only they would acknowledge it, just one of them, and be honest about it. This will pass, and you and me will still be together and happy. And what can they do anyway? At most, dismiss me from the army – and the party. So what? Of course, it won't be much fun, but it's out of our control. I can still find work anywhere.'

That's the kind of person he was. A good soul. But I just couldn't be comforted. My thoughts kept circling round in tangles, looking for a way for me to save Aarno.

I finally came up with a solution. With as much cheerfulness as I could muster, I said resolutely, 'Listen, Aarno. Say you'll do this now! If you don't, you will make me even more unhappy. Let me move back to Kondopoga. Oili's brothers will find me an apartment and a job soon enough, for sure.'

Aarno was furious and shouted, 'Never! Not in a million years! I'll be damned if I don't get to choose who I want as my wife. You're not going anywhere. If Kari were to come back, he could claim you, but I will let my fists speak if someone else tries to take you.'

'But it would be easier for me than dealing with all of this. I could be content knowing I did the right thing, and you wouldn't be upset about me forever. This will not be the end of it, and you know it as well as I do.'

But Aarno looked so insanely ferocious that it wasn't worth continuing. Besides, I knew deep down he wasn't just going to give up. All I could do was wait for what was to come.

In fact, a long time passed without any news. One evening, though, it was raised at a party meeting at the battalion school – that is, at the lowest level of the party hierarchy. I was so anxious waiting for Aarno to come home that night. I could hardly believe my eyes when I saw him in the doorway, all smiles. I figured he was trying to shield me from the outcome, which annoyed me, so I asked, 'How did it go? I expect they discharged you on account of your attempt to conceal ...'

'You what? The meeting went very well. I mean, everyone was shouting over the top of each other, but, in the end – just a reminder. They will make a note in my party membership card.'

'Come on, give me some more details.'

'I don't feel like it! I'm sick of the whole process, continually picking it over. From what I can gather, there was a final decision by the Committee of the Regions which has been rubber-stamped.'

There was something not right about how happy he looked, the poor boy; I knew it was a sign of how nerve-wracking he'd found it.

The affair didn't just fizzle out. Was it too much for them to deal with, or did the local party machinery not have enough real issues to be getting on with? Now it was taken up by the troops' party assembly. The same nonsense, the same tense, detailed questions. The debate about whether Aarno was unable to choose between his party and his woman was straight away designated as 'wrongly formulated'. Some were on Aarno's side, but plenty of others saw our marriage as a useful target at which to direct all of their righteous proletarian anger. After some commotion and hustle and bustle, the meeting passed a resolution: it was a 'warning'. According to the warning, Aarno lacked class vigilance and a Bolshevik outlook in the way he organised his affairs. It was recorded in his party membership card.

After this meeting, we breathed a sigh of relief, thinking the matter to be finally resolved. Some of the Finnish commanders still looked at us with disdain, and I was saddened, but Aarno just seemed amused.

Once more, Toivola summoned Aarno. He issued a strict order to cut me off from all previous acquaintances. But how could that be done? My network included most of those commanders I used to see when I was with Kari. Further, though, under the threat of falling foul of the party, Toivola issued an order to ensure that I was no longer in correspondence with anyone in Finland – not my parents, nor with any other former acquaintances.

That pierced me to the heart. I cried myself to sleep that night despite all Aarno's attempts at consolation. It was just such a deliberate act of cruelty to deny me contact with my own child and parents, all with the wave of his hand.

'Did you tell them Poju is there with my parents?' I asked.

'I told them that ages ago. All we can do now is obey because I gave my word. But let's just let all this hue and cry pass by; it'll all blow over in time.'

What choice did I have? There was Poju, so far away with my mother and father, wondering why my letters had stopped coming. In the end, they must have thought I was dead. What other reason could there have been for my silence?

18

August 1935

One evening in late August, I was waiting at the usual time for Aarno to return home but he was late. When he arrived he looked tired and depressed. I quickly heated up the food, laid the table, and told him to eat, assuming he'd just had a long tiring day without a break to eat. I will never forgive myself for being so blind.

He barely touched his food; he just went and lay down, sighing all the while.

'Kaarina, finish clearing up and come here. I'm so tired.'

Still my instincts failed to alert me that the cause of his fatigue lay deeper. I did go to him, though, but only to carefully pull a blanket over him. I briefly let my lips touch his thick hair, and in my mind I brushed bad thoughts aside.

'No, now you go to sleep. You look like a horse that's been ridden for too long. I'll carry on sewing for a bit.'

In the morning, while we were still in bed, Oili popped in with her daughter and her brother's wife. 'Never mind Toivola's orders,' I thought, being pleasantly surprised. 'Oili's my friend and I will receive her, regardless of whatever Toivola says.'

We had so much to talk about. We didn't even notice how silent Aarno was. I earnestly told my friend, who listened intently, all about the fuss our marriage had caused. I ended the story by sharing my fear that Aarno might still lose his party membership card because of me, and that he would then certainly be a marked man in this country.

I remember Aarno getting up, looking strange but trying to appear happy. Despite Oili being there, he wrapped his arms around me, lifted my chin and looked into my eyes: 'And that's what you were afraid of, wasn't it? But you weren't to know last night that I have in fact been expelled from the party. Well, don't take it so seriously now; you're not going to faint in my arms – I'll hold you.'

So the dismissal came after all! What sort of a person must I be to drag my husband into disaster right after getting married? I burst into sobbing tears, my head on Aarno's broad chest. Oili began weeping, too, out of sheer compassion. Aarno's grip tightened, and his gaze was hard as steel looking somewhere far across Lake Onega.

Long gone was the joy of Oili's visit; like a prisoner I walked with her around the city. In silence, we both pondered our own fortune, her thoughts far away somewhere near Novosibirsk, where Urho was working at the time – an innocent deportee, without hope – my pain just as deep fearing for Aarno's future. Fear made that future so bleak that it cast a bitter spell over our confidential friendship.

The Commission, partly comprised of the highest commanders in Leningrad and the local army, had been served up a truly exquisite catch in the shape of our marriage.

Irklis,[14] a 'squeaky-clean Bolshevik', a devotee of Lenin's great cause and a son of the proletariat, had become Karelia Party secretary, and old Rovio[15] had had to withdraw to somewhere in the countryside, branded 'a Moor who had done what was required of him'. Soon after, Edvard Gylling[16] disappeared, too; his work alongside Rovio was now characterised as 'a tilt towards nationalism in bourgeois Finland'. Irklis brandished a big stick and made sure everyone knew he was coming. And the newspapers, led by Red

---

14 Petr Irklis (1887–1937), Karelian Party secretary from August 1935 to July 1937.
15 Kustaa Rovio (1887–1938) (also known as Gustav Ravelin), Karelian Party secretary from June 1929 to August 1935.
16 Edvard Gylling (1881–1938), leader of Soviet Karelia from 1920 to 1935.

August 1935

Karelia, fell over themselves to lick his boots, chanting the sacred communist mantra until it made you sick.

The men changed. Some were imprisoned. Everywhere the great proletarian broom wielded by Irklis swept places and people before him. Even in the cosy higher echelons no one was sure of their position. Aatto, too, sitting in his teacher's house where we sometimes met of an evening, would say, in his semi-serious way, while his sweet wife was serving food: 'I, too, wish I had written a little less. It was not always so carefully considered.'

The same fear affected each one of us to some degree. Party dismissals were coming thick and fast and it was an anxious wait to see who would be next.

No wonder Aarno got expelled. After all, the affair was still so fresh, and besides, in the eyes of the Russians, Aarno was too young to be a commander in the Petrozavodsk garrison. And the Commission needed to point to some results of its clean-up work.

The Commission called on Aarno to lodge a complaint and divorce me, but my courageous darling just took offence and shook his head. No, he would never do that. Would he injure an innocent, demoralised, suffering woman – never! On the contrary, via the battalion commander he sent a petition to the upper ranks, in which he plainly requested his discharge from the Red Army altogether, arguing that, now he wasn't a member of the party, he could no longer enjoy the trust of the army.

The entire Petrozavodsk command team was astonished by all the new twists and turns and, of course, decided that I must have some part to play in it. But I wasn't involved in any of this. I didn't even know about the condition attached to the party dismissal – a recommendation to seek a divorce. In fact, Aarno needlessly hid the information from me, out of a fear of embittering me. He was so confident in those days, so calm and a little serious, but delicately tender and comforting.

The commander of the battalion wouldn't let the petition go any further, and for weeks it just sat in his in-tray. But Aarno didn't give up, and finally the paper was sent on. He just never got a reply.

The old platoon was losing men at a rate of knots while bursting at the seams with new blood. People were flooding from the plateaus of Inner Russia, the barracks were filling up, and tents for the crew were being erected in the yards, despite it being nearly autumn.

Our neighbour Lasse was the first to receive his discharge from the army. It came as a complete surprise. We might have expected transfers, either the troop as a whole or as individuals, but not discharges. Lasse was really upset and roared bitterly in his boyish way.

The next night, some important Finnish civilians were imprisoned. Other commanders were dismissed during the day. So things were progressing at a mad pace, but where to? The whispering wind wouldn't say.

19

Mid-October 1935

On 17 October, a Saturday evening, we had a social gathering at our place with a few of the commanders. It was a crowd that all knew each other well and often reciprocated as hosts.

I had just been to the sauna with my neighbour Tonja, and I was a bit anxious about my young friend's 'little visitor', which was apparently due any day. The men got the playing cards out but had to play by themselves while we women concerned ourselves with the issue at hand. The evening passed by pleasantly enough, although occasionally I saw Tonja biting her lip with the pain, as her contractions had just begun to kick in.

Just before midnight, we were all startled by a loud knock on the door. A militia captain and a lieutenant appeared in the doorway, along with a Russian commander who lived in our building. Speaking in Russian, they asked for my husband. I figured this might just be a chance visit because some of them were passing by so I didn't pay attention to the conversation – until I heard something in unmistakable Finnish: 'May I search you first?'

'Please go ahead,' I heard Aarno say.

He placed himself in front of one of them, and the militia man began to feel his trouser and chest pockets, patting him here and there.

It still hadn't occurred to me that we were being subjected to a home inspection, and I was smiling as I watched. I imagined we were having one of those so-called 'parasite inspections' that I had heard about, managing to ignore the fact that such inspections were performed by medical personnel and usually at train stations, maybe on trains, but never in your home. Only once I saw a glimpse of these people's ID documents did the truth finally dawn on me.

I can't really describe exactly what my mind was thinking right then. I watched the inspection dispassionately, from the margins, like it was a bad dream. My heart felt like it was encased in iron armour which made it hard to breathe. This was the same rigorous inspection as I'd been subjected to back in Leningrad, but this time no tears welled up. This was a second occurrence, and one that my instincts had told me was coming – and here it was.

Finally, the inspectors were done. Their catch was a small one: a couple of photos of Vierto in the suit pocket of one of the commanders and, oddly enough, the first volume of Kautsky's *Forerunners of Modern Socialism* – the second volume was left in peace on the shelf. It was a very old copy and I had no idea how it had ended up on my bookshelf.

Sitting himself at the table, the militia captain prepared a report on the incident, documenting who was present:

Mäki, Riku	commander,	from here,	party member
Jalas, Taisto	"	"	"
Viima, Toivo	"	"	"
Erkkilä, Leo	"	"	no
Halme, Lasse	"	"	"
" , Tonja		commander's wife	youth division
Rautio, Norma	"	"	no
Kivelä, Kaarina	"	"	"

Everyone! Aarno put his thick coat on and for some reason asked, 'Can I at least say goodbye to my wife?'

The militia captain shrugged, which could have been interpreted as anything.

Mid-October 1935

'Kaarina, you mustn't cry – please don't cry. This will all be sorted out, it's got to be!'

But I wasn't even crying.

I felt a sharp pain in my shoulders from the strength of Aarno's final embrace; and, yes, off he went, just like before when Kari disappeared from my life. I was alone again.

As we were saying our farewell to Aarno, the militia were busy in the Halmes' quarters, their intentions the same. Lasse and Tonja went to their room with them. The same questions were thrown at Lasse and the same arrest papers. I could hear Tonja's voice echoing in pain through the thin boarded wall as she obeyed out of fear and showed the inspectors everything she had in her home. In the end, she threw herself on her bed, the contractions no doubt wracking her entire body, and shouted hysterically, 'Oh Lasse, Lasse! What am I going to do?'

Poor Lasse. How agonising for him to be taken off to prison at this time, his young wife, pregnant with his first child, calling for help.

'Believe me, Tonja, I haven't done anything; I'm innocent. I'll get away soon. Kaarina will help you in the meantime.'

'Yes, yes, I know you're innocent, but I'm in pain and I'm afraid to be left on my own,' shrieked the girl in response.

The inspection continued in its cold and dispassionate way. It was not until the end when wives said goodbye to husbands that the NKVD[17] men showed any sign of embarrassment.

Lasse's hat and coat were still in our quarters. He came to retrieve them and said goodbye to us, looking each one of us straight and true in the eye. He seemed so young.

'Boys, don't think anything bad about me,' he said, his voice trembling like a child, then dissolving into tears. Turning to me, he grabbed my hand and blurted out, 'I know this is hard for you too, Kaarina, but please try to help Tonja.'

---

17 The GPU was merged with the OGPU (Soviet Security and Political Police) in 1934 to form the NKVD.

After a final nod to everyone, he was gone, with the door slammed behind him. And that became his fate: an only child, a boy raised by the shores of Lake Näsijärvi.

A few months later, Lasse's mother, who lived in the forest in Karelia, received a letter from her son. She responded to it immediately, sending a package. But it got sent back. It wasn't until three years had passed before she received another letter, which included the lines 'I have been rather ill here, and when it's dark I am completely blind. If I could just get a little bit of fat to eat, maybe my vision would improve. How is Tonja and what do we have: a boy or a girl?'

Mother replied, but once again the letter came back. It was not until 1939 that her enquiries were answered, informing her that Lasse had already died in a prison camp on 19 July 1938. And that's the story of Lasse.

'The joy of being a parent,' Lasse's mother would say. 'Where's the joy? You raise them up to the best of your ability, you wait to see what becomes of them and then you don't even know where he's been buried.'

But let me continue my story.

After Lasse had left with the militia, Tonja's wailing became even more plaintive. I brought her into our quarters and tried my best to reassure the poor girl overcome by fear.

The other boys and Norma formed the miserable remnant of the evening's party.

'Make a note of the time, boys,' I said, 'and see how often Tonja's contractions are occurring. If they get more frequent, you have to help me get her to the hospital somehow.'

Tonja lay down and someone placed a watch on the table. Tonja had stopped crying by now, and was gaping at the ceiling, her eyes wide. The contractions were apparently becoming less frequent so there was no need to worry about getting to the hospital just yet. A disinterested observer might have found our little group amusing to look at, so solemnly did we sit there.

We heard Volkova's clock striking from behind the other wall. The boys got up, although Toivo Viima stayed behind in case he was

Mid-October 1935

needed. The others said their goodbyes and tried to mutter something reassuring. I could see how fear for their own safety was eating them up inside: after all, their names were also on the papers of that terrifying organisation.

Tonja fell asleep. I stayed awake all night thinking about the past and fearing for the future.

20

Mid to Late October 1935

The next day, Sunday, a high-ranking 'three-poles-on the collar' NKVD man, acting all sweet and kind, came to see Tonja. He had apparently heard about the previous day's incident and her condition. He asked her to calm down and said there was no cause to be nervous, and that the matter would be resolved soon. Such mental distress would only harm the her own health and that of her unborn child.

I was outraged by this transparent pretence. If they were so sincere and concerned, why did they allow the previous day's incident to happen in the first place, for heaven's sake? They knew exactly what they were doing: the NKVD would never abduct someone unless it was planned. Anyway, they could have postponed the arrest; Lasse wasn't going anywhere while waiting for the birth of his child. Doesn't a woman suffer enough when giving birth without having more pain arranged for her?

Tonja was allowed to write a few words to her husband; the commander promised to take them to him personally by hand. He also urged Tonja to send Lasse the good news as soon as she'd given birth.

So that's exactly what Tonja did, and I left a note at the NKVD with the name clearly written on it. But, all the same, three years later the father was still asking, 'What did we have?'

Tonja spent that day in the grip of irregular contractions, pacing back and forth in my room, rubbing her aching back and sides. My little darling 2-year-old Pirjo toddled after her, pressing on her sides with her hands as well, imitating the 'ow, ow, ow's. Every now and then she remembered to run and knock on the door, shouting just as she did when Aarno used to come home, 'Daddy, come and sit with "Pijjo" to eat.'

But Daddy wasn't going to come.

At his wife's behest, Leo Erkkilä came to check on me and Tonja. He had news. The previous night, some more commanders had been imprisoned, and this time they'd got a real catch. Besides Aarno and Lasse, Koivisto, the assistant chief of staff, and Commander Laaksonen had both now been arrested. Nine commanders had reportedly been taken in Olonets. Someone had called their relatives from there and, using veiled words, told them what had happened. Also, a dozen or more people were imprisoned on Hiilisuo Farm in connection with the poisoning case.

I need to explain about Hiilisuo ...

Among the American Finns recruited to the Soviet Union were agricultural people. Many very wealthy farmers sacrificed the wealth they had accumulated for their retirement, sold their farms or simply left them and gave their all – their money, their labour and themselves – to the 'only homeland of the working class'. About 8km outside Petrozavodsk, the government designated a large, swampy area of land, not really suitable for the purpose, to be cleared and made into a Soviet farm. Many American Finns gladly joined, putting into it the money and agricultural machinery they had brought with them. Work was begun immediately; the land was ditched and cleared, and, considering all the great sacrifices that had been made, expectations for the future were high.

The farm's herd was established by dint of funding from a lonely bachelor. He was given permission to go to Finland and buy some good East Karelian cattle and a few horses out of his own pocket. On that fateful day of 17 October 1935, the cowherds feeding the cattle inadvertently gave them the wrong powder – one containing arsenic instead of the usual feed powder, with the result that within thirty minutes, eighty animals were lying with their legs sticking straight

Mid to Late October 1935

out; the vet couldn't do anything. Careless handling of the containers was the cause of the catastrophe. There followed a string of detentions, investigations, long years of imprisonment and deportations. The management of the Hiilisuo Soviet Farm were immediately branded as *kulaks* – vermin – its members accused of being 'large-scale farmers'[18] and their presence in the country characterised as a plot to undermine the well-being of Soviet society.

So that's why Aarno's captives, the militiamen, were working on behalf of another organisation, the NKVD: the latter didn't have enough men of its own to deal with everything.

It was late Sunday night when I took Tonja to the maternity ward. A frail little girl was born to her on Monday night. The young mother made rapid progress to recovery. In her notes, which she sent to me daily via the nurse, a mother's happiness shone through, as did her sense of hope for Lasse.

I was allowed to be at peace on my own at home, no visitor daring to disturb me. My Russian neighbours were downright afraid to talk to me – at least that's the impression I got. But then Vera, the young wife of a Moscow commander-in-chief, broke the ice. She came up to me courageously and said, 'Karnja Karlovna – you mustn't feel so bad! Today, you're crying. Ah! But it might be me tomorrow.'

I was taken aback by what she said. Maybe that's just how it was now? It wasn't just about your nationality. Vera, in those simple words, was expressing the shared fear of so many across the whole of Russia.

After Vera, several other commanders and their wives followed suit. Admittedly, they did not put it into words, but they would greet me more heartily than before.

The small house next door was inhabited by a sweet old railroad worker couple and their grown-up daughters, one of whom was married to a man who was an engineer. They had a cow. All this time, I had been allowed to buy evening milk from them for my Pirjo. After Aarno's arrest, that kind elderly mother came over and invited me to

---

18 'Large-scale farmers' refers to individuals attempting to benefit themselves and not the community.

hers for tea; the whole family was at home at the time. Their sympathy for me was so deep and heartfelt that it brought tears to my eyes on more than one occasion. Pirjo was passed from one lap to the next while she devoured a variety of delicacies.

As I was leaving, the old lady told me, 'My husband also served for seven years and didn't know why. The kids were in school and I was like you now.'

So she understood what we had in common. But now it was my turn to follow this familiar but difficult path.

The Finns in Petrozavodsk were much more cautious than those in Leningrad. Or were the fortunes of the proletarian class — the great hope of the Soviet nation — more precarious in a vigilant small town like this, compared to a city of a million, in which there was less danger of denunciation?

One family that did cut off all contact with me on account of that lack of 'class vigilance' was that of Commander Rautio. Norma no longer dared to come and babysit Pirjo for me when I needed to run to the maternity ward to take milk or my letters to Tonja. The last time I saw them, I was greeted by the sight of a young couple diligently destroying letters — just in case. If they were going to have a home inspection at least it would be over more quickly without any innocent love letters. Rautio tried to put on a show of bravery when he finally dared to speak to me. Without holding back, I told that coward where to go.

21

Late October 1935

A week later, there I was, sitting alone in the dark, depressed, while Pirjo slept. So, when Aune Lahti turned up, it was like a gift sent from above to ease my loneliness. She still hadn't graduated, but was completing her final year at the university's Department of Biology, planning to graduate as a teacher of physics and chemistry. Aune was a slender, blonde girl from northern Finland who had moved from Sweden to Karelia in 1926 with her mother and four siblings after her father's death.

I scarcely had time to tell her about the recent events when Toivo Viima – one of the commanders who had been at our place on the night of Aarno's arrest – burst in. He was originally from Finland as well. He made his point directly: 'It's just plain cowardice to pretend to disown your old friends when it's a safe bet that your every move is being logged anyway in the notebooks of a certain organisation.'

Aune said to me, equally directly, 'You're not to blame for any of this. I thought that before and I still think so – and especially now that you're on your own and so unhappy.'

'But,' I replied, 'think about it, though! You're both in a pretty good position right now: one of you a prospective teacher and one of you a commander. And me: now I'm a "double widow". I just don't want you to get into trouble on account of me.'

'Dear Kaarina, I'm not a child,' replied the aspiring teacher.

Aatto's young American-born wife, a teacher of biology and English at the Agricultural Technical School, also came by that night offering a sincere promise of support. She kindly implored me to move into their place while Tonja was in hospital. Of course, I wasn't going to be a burden for them; I could keep them company and tell stories. Aatto rebuffed my notion that Aarno had been incarcerated because of me.

'There must be a deeper cause than that. If he's innocent, he'll get out. Then again, a guilty man is not worth getting all concerned about.'

As the discussion turned to the imprisonments being imposed on all these Finns, he transformed into a true Soviet patriot, saying, 'In any case, come what may, the main thing is that the Soviet Union survives. Nothing else should really matter.'

Hmm! Talk is cheap: you haven't been caught in the thick of it yet, I thought. You can't make this faith of yours resonate with me any more, like you could during those prosperous times back in Finland. It's thanks to you that my child and I are now revelling in all this delight – you, the fiery-eyed recruiters whose visions I listened to and believed in, just like all the thousands of others, until I saw what things were really like.

But, being wiser now, I tried to keep my mouth shut. I didn't want to end up in Siberia and I didn't want to be separated from my child. It was crazy to think that I once imagined that I could grow here, find inner enlightenment and evolve. If only you, Red graduate and teacher, knew how my growth has actually been stunted and reversed. Sometimes I wish I could speak to a sensitive group of young Finns yearning for something beautiful, just as you and many others like you once did. But I would be saying something rather different. I would speak up and tell the truth about my own life, my own experiences; and the brutal reality would surely shock you and all the others trying to sprinkle the Soviet gold dust and enthuse about the secure, happy lives of its children. Just look at my Pirjo, so weak and fragile as a breath of wind.

Late October 1935

I simply never get an opportunity to share these truths, to put right those stories that you and so many others from the Finnish Communist Party like to tell. You can rest easy, though: your Eden is isolated like an island prison in the middle of an ocean. Only a few find their way back from here.

* * *

Tonja left the hospital feeling pretty weak. We decided to live together in my quarters primarily for financial reasons, but it was more pleasant like that anyway. Baby Terttu was a quiet and frail child who never enjoyed a day's health in all of her short life. Tonja's time was spent resting and feeding her girl; she remained strangely weak for a long time. I washed the baby's clothes every day and took great delight in bathing her. We shared everything and our financial situation began to improve. I was getting more sewing jobs from my neighbours and other Russians, and that further improved our situation. Visits from acquaintances were rare: Lasse's cousin visited with his family every now and then, as did Aune and Toivo. Who could have imagined that those faithful friends of mine who comforted me would soon find happiness together? Their own fairy tale was just beginning back then.

As for me, I began the difficult task of getting hold of Aarno's pay cheques. He had been thinking about my lack of funds even while languishing in Leningrad Prison and had succeeded in giving me power of attorney. Twice I tried to put this through via the NKVD in Petrozavodsk, but to no avail. So I took it to Aarno's battalion headquarters on Gogol Street, but had no success there either and was told to come back later. I ended up having to drag myself there over and over again. There was no shortage of explanations: the cashier was on sick leave; some other permission in Leningrad had to be sought; the order hadn't come down from the right authority. Then they began to demand evidence about why and for how long Aarno had been imprisoned. Of course, the NKVD wouldn't issue me with any such paper, even though I went in and asked for it myself. It took a fierce struggle, constant requests and persistent effort – typical Finnish determination and perseverance having a lot to do with it – before I could finally draw down the salary.

Meanwhile, the Finnish commanders were being transferred. They were sent either individually or in groups here and there all over the enormity of Russia, most to Siberia, or else on one or other side of the Middle Urals. There they were confined to the sidelines, seen as unreliable. They were kept well away from any border areas. Then, in 1938, they began to receive new transfer orders, this time at the behest of the NKVD, to even safer places: up to fifteen years in prisons and concentration camps.

22

December 1935

In early December, I received a letter from Oili telling me she was going to be deported from Leningrad:

> I thought it was some nonsense when I got the summons from the militia, but when I got there they took my passport and I was ordered to leave the city within ten days. I complained, but what was the use if neither the company party secretary nor the leader nor the union representative would dare to sign the complaint. Eero is allowed to stay – he'll be 19 soon. I swapped my room and moved into the little one next door so that Eero wouldn't have to pay such a high rent, and so the Housing Committee can't put another occupant in with him due to the size of the room. Everything has to be thought about now. I am trying to get to Khibiny, where some other Finnish deportees have gone, or so I've heard. But first I'll go to Kondopoga to say goodbye to my brothers, despite all the threats. Come to Petrozavodsk Station on 24 December (is that Christmas Eve, Kaarina?) so I can say goodbye to you. You will come, won't you?

I read the letter in shock. Oh – this land of opportunity! And now this!

In the darkness of Christmas Eve morning, I stumbled into the station to find Oili and her little Aija. Oili said, 'So this is what it's come to now.

Let's see how much longer they leave you in peace. There's no point even crying any more, you know? All you can do is dance to their tune.'

'Do you even have any money?' I asked.

'Yes, I've got my salary. But I think my brothers will be able to help me out a little. You should come to Kondopoga tonight so we can talk. Who knows whether we'll ever get the chance to meet again?'

I promised to come and so we parted ways. That afternoon, I rushed to the train station with my little girl. Because it was Christmas Eve, I was consumed by thoughts of Poju back in Finland. They have a proper Christmas celebration there. I was worrying what they must all be thinking about my lack of communication: I hadn't written a single word to them since April. And yet Aarno had been imprisoned in the end anyway. But at least Poju would be having some Christmas fun. This little one in my arms: would she ever get to experience childish joy like that?

Oili's brothers and their wives gave me a warm welcome, uninvited guest though I was. Before long, a joyful babble filled up this jolly Finnish home.

'Kaarina, you should go and stay with Ester for a while in Leningrad: she keeps mentioning it. You could sew things for her and for the children. What difference is it going make where you are? You would be able to see your friends there.'

Oili's suggestion sounded appealing; I decided to think about it.

I got home to find little Terttu seriously ill. Tonja had moved back to her quarters for fear of losing her room now she had recovered from childbirth. The child was crying quietly with a fever; we assumed she would get over it.

One day, a strange man appeared in our doorway and, in a stern voice, asked, 'Are Tonja Halme and Kaarina Kivelä here, two former commanders' wives?'

On receiving an affirmation, he announced that we had to move out of our apartments. The military was no longer going to take care of us, and the city's municipal department needed the rooms.

Tonja was very agitated and gave the man some food for thought in plain Russian: 'You can get the hell out of here but we're not moving

December 1935

unless you get us both a new apartment. And you just try driving two little kids and their mothers into the freezing December weather. Go on! Just try if you dare!'

What else could he do then but leave?

A few days later, early in the morning of 3 January, Tonja came to my quarters in her nightgown and collapsed gently onto a chest beside the door, crying, 'Terttu is dead!'

I hurried past her and found a small lifeless body in her bed. Tonja was keening bitterly: 'Two-and-a-half months! That's all the time Terttu had the strength for. Oh, why wasn't she allowed to live? Why? Why?'

Yes. Why wasn't she given more time? Perhaps gentle Fate acted for the best; forever going to sleep while still so young, she was saved from so much. I stroked the child's dark curls and closed her eyes.

Alerted by Tonja's crying, Vera came over and immediately covered both our mirrors with a cloth and closed the curtains: the proper Russian custom when death has visited a house. She forbade Tonja to cry: 'Your child is finally happy now.' Again, these were time-worn words of consolation, from way before the Soviet era, even though they were being uttered by someone born after the Revolution.

I made a small gauze nightgown out of Tonja's thin blouse, decorated it with lace and narrow silk ribbons, and, after washing the tiny body, I dressed her for the last time.

When Tonja was preparing herself to report the death, our bailiff reappeared: 'Yes, you do in fact have to move out. Go to the municipal department and they can organise an apartment for you, somewhere or other.' He sounded tetchy and pompous.

'Is that so?' Tonja replied, the anger burning through her tears. 'We are not moving – at least not today. My child died this morning. Her body is still warm! Let me bury my dead in peace. We'll go afterwards.'

The man simply stared at this beautiful, raging young Karelian wife, crazy with grief, but this just made Tonja more agitated. She exclaimed, 'Do you not understand what I mean by "go away"?! Or are you going to make me leave my house carrying my dead child in my arms?'

The man finally turned and went. Tonja burst into a desperate cry.

'I can't take it any more, Kaarina. It just gets more and more horrible. And now my Terttu is dead. At least they can't evict her.'

Yes, nothing was going to upset Terttu any more.

Terttu's procession was small in number. We walked across the city, Tonja's sister bearing the small coffin using a wide piece of clothing. At Soroka Cemetery, we lowered the coffin into the bosom of Mother Earth with no words of remembrance, just Tonja's low moaning accompanying the clang of the shovel.

Funerals in the Soviet Union mostly had none of the beautiful, sad and festive ceremony that is customary everywhere else. If there was a speech, it was because there was some dignitary present, delivering the usual socialist diatribe by the graveside. Other less favoured mortals were buried with no blessing other than the weeping of their loved ones.

Grandad in 1936. This picture was taken on Hämeentie – a main road in Helsinki. (Hyrske family album)

Grandad with his own grandparents, c.1940. (Hyrske family album)

Grandad and Kaarina. (Hyrske family album)

Bombed buildings in Helsinki, 1939, by photographer Hugo Sundström. A cluster bomb fell on Aurorankatu on 1 December 1939. This image illustrates how the Soviets did bomb Helsinki and other cities, despite telling their people that only border areas were bombed. (Finnish Heritage Agency, CC BY 4.0)

Photographs of the devastation of the Helsinki bombings taken without permission by Kurt Karlsson, head of Pori civil protection, during his command in Helsinki during 1942–43. (Satakunta Museum, CC BY 4.0)

Photograph of Kaarina's house and family in Nukuttalahti, *c.*1940. (Hyrske family album)

Kaarina and her goat, early 1940s. (Hyrske family album)

A family of three in Nukuttalahti, *c*.1940. (Hyrske family album)

Äänislinna, parade of the anniversary of the seizure of Petroskoi on 1 October 1942. (Finnish Heritage Agency, CC BY 4.0)

Matti Hyrske (Poju), the author's son, in his military uniform, and with his military unit, early 1940s. (Both Hyrske family album)

Scene of the first meeting of the Allied Control Commission in Berlin, 5 June 1945. Left to right, seated: French General de Lattre de Tassigny (profile); British Field Marshal Sir Bernard Montgomery; Russian Marshal Gregor Zhukov; American General Dwight D. Eisenhower. (Photo 12 / Alamy Stock Photo)

Kaarina and her daughter Pirjo. This photograph was taken after her memoir was written. (Military Museum, CC BY 4.0)

Kaarina. (Military Museum, CC BY 4.0)

23

January 1936

After we had laid the tiny departed one to her final rest, it was time for us to follow our bailiff's orders. We went to the city municipal department to find out more. It was a typical Soviet office, full of desks, even down to the customary lazy and rude staff. The man to whom we presented our case snapped at us as he asked for more information.

'Er, well, your husbands have already got an apartment,' he said spikily.

'It looks like they just didn't bother to give it to their wives,' snarled someone nearby, and the whole office burst out laughing.

Tonja said firmly that this was no laughing matter, and where our men had ended up had been nothing to do with us. The man gave her an embarrassed glance and quickly pushed a piece of paper in front of us, saying, 'Go and take a look and then come back here.'

Written on the piece of paper were the addresses 53 Kalini Street and 49 Anohin Street.

We hurriedly made our way to the first one. This was reserved for me: a small narrow room of 9m², with a window facing the morning sun.

'Good,' I said. 'This will do for Pirjo and me. Now let's go and have a look at your room, Tonja.'

No. 49 Anohin Street was an ancient, dilapidated house, which was leaning to one side. The section reserved for Tonja was about 3m² and situated in a corridor.

'I'm not living here,' she said immediately.

However, in the end, she had to, even though she was able to lodge a complaint in perfect Russian to both the public procurer of the republic and of the city. The former told her she'd be best advised to move without delay, as the house we were living in was going to be handed over by the army to a school for use as a dormitory. There was no option. The city lawyer snapped at Tonja on her way out: 'You should be grateful for getting any kind of room. You try putting up a fight and see where it gets you.'

Neither was my move as straightforward as it seemed at first. I went with Tonja to see Laukkanen, the deputy chairman of the city council – Tonja was still pushing for a better apartment as well. Laukkanen seemed like a reasonable person. He explained that the municipal department didn't have any right to hand over the room reserved for me to anyone else. But that was exactly what they'd already tried to do. Laukkanen called the municipal department, argued with them in Russian and slammed the phone down in anger. We told him how the municipal department had joked about our husbands, and Laukkanen insisted that we lodge a complaint about the matter, in Finnish if necessary. Such behaviour was utterly indefensible, he said. So we did, and we brought our complaint back to Laukkanen. Some time later, Tonja received a reply in the post telling her the case had been dropped because it was 'a completely unfounded and false accusation, which is denied by the entire staff'.

'Oh really, you dogs?' said Tonja, bitterly. 'So we were lying, were we? Well, you've managed to make it go away by lying yourselves, the whole lot of you. There's nothing I can do on my own while I don't count as an eligible witness because of my lack of Russian. I suppose I can count myself lucky that they didn't slap a prison sentence on me.'

On 16 January, I arrived by horse-drawn carriage at my new apartment. The door appeared to be double-locked, with the top lock emblazoned with a city council seal. It's fortunate that I didn't just pull at it and break it. I had to hump my possessions into the hallway and then scurry back to Laukkanen. He promised to get permission from the president of the Supreme Court of the Republic to get the

January 1936

door properly opened. This request was going so high up that he enquired whether meanwhile I could find somewhere for me and my girl to stay for one night.

At the agreed time in the morning, I went back to my apartment in the hope of taking possession of it. I arrived to find a representative of the city council and a locksmith, with the militia arriving behind me. The door was opened and a report was written. But my face dropped when the city representative politely insisted that I leave and closed the door behind me again, dropping the key in his pocket. Apparently, this was by order of Laukkanen!

In Laukkanen's office, I was raging and gave him both barrels with a completely unrehearsed tirade. Evicting me from an apartment with a child in the icy January weather? Making me run back and forth? As a Finn, did he not think that was an evil thing to do to a woman and child? Or did he think he was doing the right thing? All my belongings were piled up outside in a passageway back there on Kalini Street, and I was not prepared to move them anywhere else on my own.

'My child is currently in the care of a doctor,' I said. 'I will get a certificate saying I am unable to care for her as a homeless person, and based on that certificate I will complain so high up until someone listens. One thing I have learnt in this country is that you don't get anywhere unless you persevere.'

'You could find a woman to move in with for the time being,' said Laukkanen tentatively.

'No. All my belongings are there. You move them if you want. I can't do anything with them now. How can you even suggest such a thing, Comrade Laukkanen?'

'Oh, for ...'s sake, have it your way,' he said at last. 'There's the key.'

Once again, grit and determination won the day! It was later that I learned that an attempt had been made to give my room to a council official, a young woman who was staying at Laukkanen's place.

Now at least I had a roof over my head. How long for? That was another matter.

In the loneliness of my new apartment Oili's entreaty to me to travel to Leningrad kept coming back to me. I would need to raise funds for the trip, but if I left it much longer it would be too late anyway. So, by 28 January, I was in Leningrad.

I was greeted by the big city's familiar noise and commotion. The happy times I had here living with Kari came flooding back to me. Could I ever be so old and so decrepit that such vivid memories as these, animated by the urban hustle and bustle, would fade?

At Ester's house, only her children were at home: Lea (15), Maire (5) and Aarre in the third grade. The joy that erupted when they saw Aunt Kaarina and her Pirjo! Lea went straight to their neighbours to call her mum and tell her we were here. But the office was busy so we couldn't find out when Ester was coming home.

I had timed my visit to Leningrad to coincide with the annual commemoration of the Finnish Revolution; that evening I would hopefully bump into all the celebrating Finns. True to my expectations, I saw a lot of familiar faces. During the intermission all my time was taken up saying hello to people. This was my Leningrad circle and they weren't downright afraid to admit they knew you, like people were back in Petrozavodsk. The evening flew by, and there was plenty to talk about.

I found Aunt Anna working in the pharmacy; she was taken by surprise to see me.

'How are you coping now that Aarno's been taken from you as well?' was her first question.

'What can you do about it, dear Aunt? You don't seem to die of a broken heart, even if they take your husband from you. You just have to keep on living.'

That evening, Eero, Oili's son, came to see me and tell me the news about his mother. Oili's brothers in Kondopoga had asked the NKVD representative if Oili could remain in Kondopoga as their responsibility. Absolutely not! An unauthorised stay could lead to very undesirable consequences. And that was immediately followed by a dispassionate order to leave the Kondopoga district within the next twenty-four hours.

All her relatives could do was help to stock Oili up for her trip north. In Khibiny, she had registered with the militia, taken a room

January 1936

in some miserable tavern and applied in vain for jobs in that unfamiliar place. A week later, tired of all her futile efforts, she had gone back to the head of the militia and asked for a transfer to Murmansk. Permission was granted and Oili wasted no time. In Murmansk her little daughter Aija fell ill. The money dwindled away and still no employment was to be had. On account of Aija's persistent fever, she was left with no alternative but to turn back despite the risk. She returned to Kondopoga and stayed with her brothers, her little Aija still seriously ill.

Ester was a Finn from St Petersburg. She had married her first husband very young and they both worked while his mother looked after the household and their two children. Her husband began to drink himself into oblivion and Ester divorced him just to bring some peace back to the household. Before long, a young Finnish naval commander living on the other side of the wall began to call on a daily basis, and soon these young people were merging their lives together. Ester's mother was furious; Arvi, the children's father, came to his senses, stopped drinking altogether, and began to beg Ester to have him back, if only for the sake of the children. When the young commander was sent on several months' secondment, he returned to hear Ester tell him she was going back to the father of her children. In fact, that decision didn't lead to much conflict; in complete mutual understanding, the three young people even sat down together for a meal to mark the separation.

A few years later, Arvi died. Ester married a Russian engineer and had her younger children by him. This marriage was never made official, however, and one day Ester heard that the engineer had married someone else far away in his new place of business — somewhere he had claimed wasn't safe for Ester and the children. It wasn't exactly fun and games, but you had to get used to what life threw at you. Admittedly, the children did get an allowance from their deceitful father, and Ester had a well-paid job so she was able to cope.

Some time later, she received an invitation from her party committee. They wanted to take her party membership card off her.

'You were the wife of Marine Commander Karppinen?'

'Well, yes, about ten years ago I was.'

'Are you aware of the verdict against your husband?'

'I heard that he was shot as a class traitor. But what has that got to do with me? I mean, we were married for less than a year.'

'Do you really have to ask? Where was your class vigilance? As a long-standing party member ...'

And that was that. Ester couldn't help but laugh about it, even though she knew the loss of her membership card was a portent of a bigger storm coming. But how could she have anticipated ten years in advance what direction a man's heart would turn, if there even had been a turn? How much did it take for a Red Army officer's head to fall? No head is as loose as that of a Red Commander.

I was worried about Pirjo. The change in climate going to Leningrad gave her three bouts of severe fever while we were there. On the basis of a medical report, Ester was allowed to extend my two-week leave to one and a half months. I tried to be useful and it occurred to me that she didn't want to lose me.

I enquired about Aarno and was told that 'investigations are ongoing'. I even tried to see the military prosecutor, but there were no more civil interviews that month.

Eero came over to us late one night. He sat for a while and then, bursting into tears, threw Oili's letter in front of me. I read that Oili's little girl had died of laryngitis. How well I understood her big brother's feelings as I tried to comfort him.

In early March I finally left Leningrad; I had already taken too much advantage of Ester's hospitality anyway. As it was, the Leningrad militia wouldn't extend the permit indefinitely either. Only if you were given a job assignment or an organisation assignment, or if you were a student, were you allowed to move to a Soviet metropolitan area as a permanent resident. A marriage could also provide that opportunity, but it was rarely a case of a simple application. Only aliens had the right to settle wherever they wanted, as long as they secured an apartment.

24

March 1936

My trip to Leningrad had drained the last of my meagre funds. Now I had to get a job and some money fast if I was going to stay alive. But that was a lot easier said than done.

'We don't need any female labour at the moment,' said the Petrozavodsk ski factory. Nor was it required at the distillery, the mica factory or in countless other factories. If you didn't have any language fluency, you could forget about the easier jobs. As for contacts and acquaintances, that was a dead end, for who dared to speak on behalf of a widow like me? The big Onega factory offered me some work loading timber, although they looked rather sceptically at my slight physique. Naturally, I tried to do as much sewing as I could, but the big artisan factory had burnt down and the work had dried up.

With no jobs forthcoming, I went straight to the Department of Children and Maternity Care of the People's Commissariat for Health of the Republic and asked them to either find a job for me or arrange some other means for my child to survive. My daughter was not going to starve: the matter had to be resolved one way or another.

'As a city inhabitant, you're the responsibility of the city council health department, not us.'

OK, fine. I went to that department and presented my case. They found me an adequate Karelian interpreter and my request was taken into consideration.

'Yes, we can give your child a place in a crèche for two weeks, but you'll have to work during that time. We can't guarantee this until we've got the Commission to check that your family situation is as you say it is.'

I was halfway out of the door when the same clerk hurried after me and said she would recommend me to the city's labour department, to see if it could manage to organise a job for me. But they couldn't get me a job either. There might be some street cleaning before long and some gardening in the spring, but nothing for the time being. Then the clerk remembered that she knew Venno, a journalist at Red Karelia, and that's where she would try to place me. She scribbled out a letter of recommendation, smiling victoriously as if I had already got the job. I already knew from experience how incredibly dubious Finnish officials in charge were about widows like me, but I went along anyway at the behest of the smiling clerk.

At the editorial office, I met a familiar-looking junior journalist who directed me to Editor-in-Chief Venno's office. A short, stocky man, he put his questions to me in a businesslike way. I didn't attempt to evade the question of my husband's whereabouts. I noticed the reporter could hardly sit still; after twitching impatiently, Venno finally blurted out, 'Who the hell would be so stupid as to hire you?'

I snapped back sourly, 'I didn't expect anything better than that from you, even if you are a Finn.'

'Well, think about how many applicants we get of all kinds. It's not like I'm running an employment agency here.'

'I never thought you were; I came here because your friend sent me.'

'She doesn't know your story. But I can call the printing department and see if they've got anything. Hello! Get Silventoinen for me, would you? Have you got any work for someone who's not got any print industry experience? No? OK, fair enough! ... As you heard, there's nothing. Go over to our canteen and find out for yourself.'

So that was the Finns' Red tribal spirit, or, rather, their 'comrade spirit'. I completely regretted going there just to be embarrassed and offended. Finding a job seemed a hopeless task. It would be best to get divorced, so if I applied for a job I could just say I was divorced and leave it at that.

I bought some paper and ran with my girl in my arms to Tonja's sister at Komsomolskaya, where I completed a divorce application,

March 1936

tears rolling down my cheeks:

To the Department of Civil Registry of the City of Petrozavodsk, from Citizen Kaarina Karlovna Kivelä.

Application.
I am petitioning for a divorce from my husband, former Junior Lieutenant Aarno Andrejevits Kivelä. He was imprisoned here in the city of Petrozavodsk on 17 October 1935, and I have not heard from him since. I will continue to use my last name Kivelä.

Petrozavodsk, 13 March 1936.
Kaarina Karlovna Kivelä

My application was accepted and a response was promised after a couple of days. I walked home wondering what Aarno would have thought about this. But he would understand if he knew the reason why, I comforted myself.

The 'Commission' that the health department had promised turned out to be a sweet Finnish lady, a kind old dear who got involved with these kinds of things to do her bit for society. It was easy to open up to her, and the nice lady promised to do her best to help me.

After she left, I took stock of my financial assets and it wasn't a pretty picture. Six roubles, not a kopek more. I had to take out a loan, but who from? There was not one single person in Petrozavodsk to whom I felt close enough to dare ask for a loan. I couldn't have asked Aatto, even though he certainly could have lent me the money. Then I remembered Oili's brothers in Kondopoga, checked the time, picked up Aarno's watch and set off to see them that same afternoon. All my life I have been wary of taking on debt; only extreme circumstances could drive me to it.

Oili was still in Kondopoga. After her daughter died, she'd just stayed put.

'Come and take me and put me in prison. I don't care. It's all the same to me,' she said.

Oddly enough, they hadn't even come looking for her.

'I finally got some information about Urho as well,' she said quietly. 'Do you remember Eino Pyy? He managed to get away and he wrote that Urho had died of flying lung disease[19] a month ago. I just want to be with Eero if I can. Anyway, I'm going to try to get to Leningrad to see him; if they don't let me, then it doesn't matter to me where I live – or if …'

'Please don't say that, Oili, this has to get easier at some point. We can't keep getting ground down for all eternity.'

But Oili just gave a short and bitter laugh as if she had lost her faith in everything.

'You carry on believing that if you want!'

When I got back to Petrozavodsk – I had managed to borrow a pretty decent sum – I hurried straight from the station to the health department. I was fortunate to meet a young girl on the street who agreed to be my interpreter.

The ruling was clear: I would get a permit entitling me to take my girl to the nearest crèche for two weeks. They told me to wait a minute. There were several clerks in the room talking in Russian to one another while glancing at Pirjo.

I couldn't follow what they said, but my interpreter told me, 'They're talking about you and Pirjo. They're wondering how Finnish mothers always look so exhausted and yet have such well-dressed children. And how well they take care of their children as well.'

I looked at Pirjo. She did look so sweet in her white jacket and cap; I'd made them from the pieces of felt from under the paper-processing machines which Oili had given me. Her brown eyes shone and her frost-reddened cheeks glowed. Who wouldn't give their child all that they could?

A young man with a briefcase stepped in, took stock of us for a moment, then came over.

'Are you Comrade Kivelä? Please check the amount,' he said and handed me three new 10-rouble banknotes. I felt myself flush bright

---

19 Pulmonary tuberculosis.

red and started to stutter. What I was trying to say was that I hadn't asked for money, let alone a measly handful of change like this. But my interpreter pushed me aside: 'Are you crazy or what? Take it when they offer it and get it signed for.'

Frustrated and embarrassed, I took the money. I could still feel my shame as I stood on the street outside. For the first time in my life, I had received welfare assistance. A few years earlier it would have been a flat refusal, but now I just had to take it. The money was really neither here nor there; it was ludicrous to offer such a small amount to someone in need. But, on the other hand, the time had come to surrender my pride and accept the futility, even though I'd struggled my way through such mixed fortunes for years.

On the same day I also got my divorce certificate; it was granted 'on reasonable grounds' and cost only 3 roubles.

The crèche on Uritski Street, where I took Pirjo, was a pleasant surprise. Rather than cold and formal, it was bright and warm, and radiated cleanliness and order. The crèche was the work of American Finns – mothers who had lived in a Western environment.

I was finally able to rush around again looking for a job. I managed to get into a craft artel,[20] which continued operating even after the fire. As a newcomer, I of course got the machine that no one else wanted, in one of the lowliest and worst-paid jobs. In my workshop, they mainly made basic underwear under an assembly-line system. I remember my first few weeks treading away on this rickety machine as fast as I could, sewing nothing but the seams of military shirt sleeves at 3 kopeks a pair. I'd put a lot of work in before I'd even earned a whole rouble. It was intensely busy, low-margin contract work that generated a terrible, ear-splitting noise in which you could hardly hear the person next to you speaking. The so-called 'Stahanovs'[21] in the group weren't very popular among the other employees, for they would create extremely long machine stitches to maximise the

---

20 A workers' cooperative for craft, artisan and light industrial enterprises.
21 Named after Alexei Stahanov whose exceptional productivity in a coalfield led to a movement promoted by the Soviet authorities in which improved organisational labour practices were financially rewarded.

number of finished items. Theirs would often get sent back unless they managed to blend them in among the items made by the more careful workers.

I soon got to know a few of the Finns and I felt relieved. I'd got some work at last. At home in the evenings, I was still diligently pedalling at my machine to earn some extra income.

Throughout the summer, I worked like a dog, with a meagre salary and not much food. When autumn came, though, a serious obstacle threatened my job. Pirjo's birthday meant she now had to move to a nursery – a facility for children over 3 years old. The crèche opened as early as 7 a.m. and you could leave your child there until 6 p.m., but the nursery didn't open until 8 a.m. and closed at 5 p.m. My job had two shifts, and I became anxious. I checked out all the nurseries on my side of the city, but they all had the same hours. There was one weekly nursery, but it was only for children who had lost their mothers or children of higher-ranking workers. Neither case applied to me.

Luckily, our interim leader put me in as an apprentice for the 'Jacket Brigade': the department making men's overcoats. It was daytime work only there, and Pirjo's nursery was very close by. I had been rescued once again.

My life was financially quite secure now. Considering everything, that was something to be grateful for. My salary was higher than it had been in the linen department and it was easier working with this Finnish crew: my co-workers were all recruited American Finns who, with a few exceptions, behaved cordially and openly towards me, and gave me advice and help.

25

Spring 1936 to Autumn 1937

So life calmed down for me, but not for my friends.

Oili wrote saying she had left Kondopoga for Leningrad. She had submitted an application to the militia, asking permission to live in the city with her son. The response was: leave the city within twenty-four hours, remain in the countryside, outside a 100km radius of the city, and send them the address she was staying at. They would then, in due course, indicate whether there had been a positive or negative response to her request.

I do not know who gave Oili the address of a farming collective somewhere out there, which, to be on the safe side, was about 280km from Leningrad. Oili travelled there to wait and wrote to me:

> I feel like a summer guest here. I sold Urho's clothes to get something to live off – no need to save them for him now. Time just stands still, but I couldn't have stayed in Kondopoga either. Have you already heard? Both my brothers were imprisoned back in the spring while I was there. Tell me: is this worth living for? And was it worth coming all this way for this?

She wrote again later, this time from Leningrad:

Eero got taken ill and Ester immediately sent me a telegram because they were afraid Eero would die. I came again with whatever defiance I had left in me; just let them try dragging me from my dying son's bedside and putting me in prison. Eero is the only one I have left. But my neighbour, Maria Andrejeva, with some help from her friends, managed to get me a month's residence permit from the militia department, at least while Eero was ill. And after Eero got better the same kind soul managed to get me a job as a cleaner at the Botanical Museum, and now they are extending my city resident's permit by three months at a time. Who knows for how long?

As soon as I'd got my divorce, I had written to Poju in Finland. I was no longer the wife of a commander in custody, and being divorced from him I couldn't cause Aarno any more harm. My dear mother immediately wrote me a moving letter in response: '... and we'd no idea that you were still alive.'

I just cannot put into words how I felt as I read the letter and looked at the photograph of the grown-up Poju. It was so good to be in touch with them again and know that they were alive and well.

★ ★ ★

In that letter and subsequent ones, they asked about Aarno; after all, he had written to them when he became their son-in-law and had received a reply. But I was careful not to even mention Aarno or his fate; I ignored such potentially controversial questions for the sake of my own peace and safety. In general, these kinds of connections with Finland were not very wise; they made things difficult for a lot of people – in fact, quite a few people dropped them altogether to stay out of trouble.

Aarno's comrade Commander Siimes came by to pass on my husband's greetings. Aarno wanted me to keep hold of his civilian clothes if possible in case he ever needed them again. Investigations still seemed to be ongoing; were they struggling to find solid evidence, or what else was prolonging it so much?

Spring 1936 to Autumn 1937

'He should be getting out of there before too long,' Siimes said in conclusion.

But it wasn't to be. Autumn passed, winter came, we moved into 1937, and yet I still waited in vain.

I decided to spend May Day bank holiday in Leningrad – Pirjo by my side, of course. Oili and Ester met us at the station. They told me that Aarno had finally received his sentence after one year and seven months in custody. So they were told, anyway. Two men who had managed to get out spoke of Aarno complaining in the next-door cell: 'So finally I've got a five-year 'secondment'. Well, well ...'

It must have been difficult digging around to come up with a sentence to pin on a former Finnish prison hunger striker. Anyway, that's all I heard – nothing via official channels.

As summer merged into autumn, a strange letter from Ester arrived. In veiled language she conveyed that she had been deported from Leningrad to some faraway corner of rural Russia:

My dear Kaarina, this is my goodbye to you, my friend. I will be travelling far away with my kids – no other choice really. This is the worst thing that could have happened for Lea – she would have been better off staying around people with brighter prospects. No point crying over spilt milk, though. Farewell, dear Kaarina and your Pirjo.

Ester and the children

I later found out that she, too, had suddenly been presented at home with an order to appear before the militia, at which point the deportation order was handed out. You had to leave within no more than ten days, on such and such a day, from such and such a platform in Leningrad, and at such and such a time. Oili had waved at the train, full of those poor unfortunates, hidden out of sight on a siding. The farewells of the deportees with their loved ones seeing them off had been heartbreaking. The only emotionless ones were the soldiers on guard moving around in the midst of it all.

I received a long and sad letter from Ester from where she'd been deported. It was a desolate steppe, clay hut shacks for accommodation and the floors just bare soil:

The children are living like pigs – there's no water for washing, even with all the tears. Our troupe is very diverse, predominantly well educated – doctors, engineers, teachers and officials. Every area of expertise is covered ...

To her female friend in Leningrad, she wrote:

... all those old pieces of bread that you end up with – my dear friend, don't throw any of them away. Dry them in the oven until they go hard – you get fine black bread. Next winter will definitely be a harsh one, and those black crackers will make a nice treat for my children.

That was the story of Ester and her children. I don't know what happened next. They were either relocated somewhere else or maybe they ended up buried on the shores of the grey steppe. Who will ever know?

★ ★ ★

On the eve of the October festivities, I got to travel to Leningrad again for a couple of days. I had been talking about how much I wanted to see my friends, and an acquaintance of mine, a Finn from Canada called Martti Varpio, got quite excited about it.

'If you promise to guide me through that chaotic stone village of Leningrad, I'll pay for your return ticket on the Strela. You might want to buy yourself some clothes: there'll be more choice there.'

'Yes, if you pay for the trip I'll organise it and take you round and be your guide. And you can stay with my friends as well and save yourself the expensive hotel fee,' I replied.

The deal was sealed there and then.

Spring 1936 to Autumn 1937

It was a pleasure to be sitting on the Strela – 'The Arrow' – the express train that ran daily from Leningrad to Murmansk and back again. There was a big difference between this high-speed train and the ordinary passenger trains, although even the Strela wasn't up to the standards of Finnish second class. The carriages of the regular Russian trains had two benches in each compartment, plus these 'shelves' on top: a rough platform to accommodate the overnight passengers who didn't have a reserved seat. The high walls separating the compartments went all the way up to the ceiling, supposedly to prevent luggage being stolen, but in fact created a cramped, prison-like environment. Everything was painted black and brown. They didn't even bear comparison with Finland's airy, bright third-class carriages, but they served their purpose here in Russia, with its dreadful, endless waves of travellers. Travelling in Russia is not a pleasure, but all the same you get the impression that everyone is constantly on the move carrying teapots and bundles. No laws or regulations can keep them in one place.

I took Martti Varpio to see Oili, where we received a warm welcome. In no time, I had heard all the latest about my friends.

'Liisi and Ilmari Urpola received a deportation order a while ago – the same thing: leave the city within ten days. They were getting ready to leave, but the night before they were due to go, Liisi was arrested. Ilmari had to travel on his own to some distant place near Frunze. Oddly enough, Toini was allowed to stay, and she took Liisi's little girl in. Now Toini has three fatherless girls in her care. Her own daughter's father has been shot, and her niece's father met the same fate. Now she has Liisi's daughter as well, whose father, apparently, has just been given a ten-year sentence. He was sent somewhere far out east.'

I heard about the sad fates of many other Finnish acquaintances as well. For some reason, Oili wasn't completely at ease with me; it looked like something was bothering her, something she was afraid to tell me.

I bided my time before expressing my concern, 'Is anything wrong with you? There's something not the same about you.'

Oili was startled and mumbled, 'It's not like that. What are you saying? Have I ever hidden anything from you before?'

'No, but there's something wrong now, isn't there? Don't deny it.'

We were alone in the room and I was feeling hurt so I felt I could speak candidly. Oili still demurred for a moment, but friendship prevailed, and she began to explain, hesitantly and almost apologetically:

'I suppose I'd better tell you, otherwise you'll only think all sorts of things. I was summoned the other day to the "Big House" on Liteyny Avenue to be interrogated on account of you. Oh yes! I went in, they took my passport off me straight away and led me down lots of corridors until I finally saw an interrogator and interpreter. They asked me about everyone – you, your parents, your first husband in Finland, Kari and Aarno – everyone. Of course, I told them what I knew – what else could I have done? After the interrogation, they left me on my own in a room for a couple of hours before the escort came to get me and gave me my passport at the front door. You couldn't believe how frightened I was; I was so frightened that the sweat was just running down off me. I was certain you'd been taken and Pirjo would be on her own. Even my own position seemed like it was at risk again; I was going crazy just at the thought of losing my passport. It was only when I received your letter that I finally calmed down.'

'But you didn't reply for months!' I said.

'No, and I won't be writing to you again, Kaarina. I made that decision when I was up there in the "Big House". Please don't feel upset about it, but it makes sense, doesn't it? We stop all correspondence, but we keep meeting like this from time to time?'

Well, well, I said to myself. I must be a very dangerous creature in the eyes of the NKVD: it seems their interest in me hasn't diminished. But why didn't they just arrest me? It puzzled me. Or maybe the time wasn't yet right for that?

Oili had recently married an old American–Finnish craftsman and was doing better financially. She and her new husband escorted me to the station and we all bid a tearful goodbye. So she thought I was going to end up in prison as well.

26

Autumn 1937

As the summer of 1937 turned into autumn, another big clean-up was being anticipated. 'Squeaky-clean' Irklis had lost his sheen and now it was his turn to vanish from the picture. A rumour persisted of his being imprisoned, but no one expected to see anything about it in the papers, like there had been when he rose to prominence on the political scene in Karelia. The broom could no longer sweep and had to be replaced.

Irklis was replaced by Matushenko, to be what Irklis had been a couple of years earlier. Via newspapers, orators and tannoys, you saw how quickly news could be broadcast about an unprecedentedly purebred Bolshevik taking control of life in Karelia.

The arrests began again, first mainly among the top echelons of the Finnish community. As far as I can recall, the old poet and translator Lauri Letonmäki took his own life. He feared that 'political errors' would be identified in the various books on Leninism and such like that he had translated into Finnish, and he preferred to surrender his own life rather than his freedom. At the turn of the year, Red Karelia was shut down by a draconian order and most of its journalists imprisoned. The Karelian-language newspaper *Sovetskoi Karelija* was established in its place, and was incomprehensible even to Karelians, even though it was supposed to be in their own language, albeit set in a Russian typeface. It didn't gain much support, just being delivered to the reading rooms, to organisations, and to some of the '100 per centers'.[22]

After they'd put most of the higher stratum behind bars, they trained their crosshairs on regular folk. Through the autumn, winter, spring and on until mid-summer the following year, NKVD men moved by night from house to house, from apartment to apartment. It was a time that everyone recalls with horror, and which, with good reason, was referenced by Finns as 'The Great Wrath'.[23] For a while in the springtime, capturing women was even in vogue. Their children were first taken to orphanages, from where they were then sent elsewhere. They were not just separated from their parents but from the entire Finnish community; soon they were integrated among the various Russian ethnicities, with no memory of their true families.

Fear of imprisonment hung over everybody's head. When midnight came, there was not much sleep to be had in the larger rental houses, with the tenants listening keenly for the big military boots stomping in the hallways, waiting to see whose door they would pass by and whose door would be fiercely pounded. Only when the echoes of footsteps finally subsided was there some peace of mind, the ability to breathe again: 'it hasn't been our turn tonight'. In the summer, some left the city altogether or spent the night somewhere else – in the woods or on the riverbank. The NKVD men would always come at night, but, if after several visits they didn't find who they were looking for, they would give up. A whole truckload of workers was taken from the ski factory in broad daylight in the middle of the working day, but other workplaces seemed to avoid such a fate.

Aku Rönkä was a young sawmill worker whom they were after, but he was out of town with his new bride. When he left the next

---

22 This is likely a reference to those who retained a 100 per cent belief in the state and its mantra.
23 In reference to the first Great Wrath (1714–21) when Russia had occupied Finland and killed or enslaved thousands of civilians including women and children. Children were taken from their families to be brought up in Russia by non-Finnish families in order to integrate them into Russian society. Later, the 1930s phenomenon became known as 'The Great Purge'.

night, he left his passport out on a shelf: his thinking was that, if they took it, that would be a sign that his time had come. That night they did indeed take the passport. Now the poor boy desperately started preparing for his departure: he got his bride to mend his clothes, put together a store of food – and, most importantly, plenty of makhorka; he left power of attorney to his bride for his payroll; and he would have resigned from his job as well, but the Russian ringmaster just laughed: 'If we all did that, what do you think would happen? I get dragged in by the NKVD all the time but they haven't kept hold of me yet.'

At the NKVD, Aku did indeed get his passport back and was told to go back to work. The ringmaster had laughed again. The food rations got eaten, the tobacco was smoked, and the boy calmed down. But one night his captors returned, and this time they took him away for real. Apparently, what annoyed the boy the most was that now he had to leave without any makhorka.

Another story tells of how the captors were looking for a man named Nousiainen. This Nousiainen was sitting drunk at a table, and the person next to him knew him only by his nickname, 'Easter', and so declared that there was no one present by the name of Nousiainen. The captors left and Nousiainen slipped off as well. Before long, the NKVD men were back and this time they were angry, having found out that Nousiainen had indeed been right in front of them. But he wasn't there now. Enraged, they grabbed someone else instead, and in the morning told him he had to go and fetch Nousiainen if he wanted his passport back. Nousiainen was found and in fact the two of them were old friends, so they spent the next couple of days drowning their sorrows before they finally surrendered themselves to the NKVD, inebriated, arms around each other's shoulders. They were told they were in no fit condition and must return when they had sobered up. So, sometime after their 'festivities', back they went: one got his passport back, the other no doubt remained in custody.

The Petrozavodsk repair works brigade was imprisoned after a workplace raid. A couple of Finnish workers managed to sneak home just so they could get a change of clothes. Their wives both hurriedly put some provisions together and mended their clothes. Paavo's wife sewed the final button on her husband's trousers, saying bitterly, 'There you are: as far as I'm concerned, you're good to go.'

A moment later, Paavo heard something and replied, 'And here come the search party.'

He wasn't wrong.

* * *

It seemed like the arrests would never end. No one was exempt from being an NKVD target. The defectors were all picked off one by one – certainly the men, including the recruited American Finns, and the commanders almost to the last man.

Norma Rautio came to see me, looking miserable, with her little 6-month-old girl. It had been her husband's turn to be imprisoned. Norma felt that there was nothing to be gained any more by shunning the relatives of prisoners, now that her turn had come. I didn't feel like trying to get my own back in this situation after what she'd done to me; instead I tried to forget the past.

One day in early July I got home from work to find Jussi, Oili's new husband, with Eero. They had come to Petrozavodsk as part of their summer holidays and were planning to visit Kondopoga as well.

'How's Oili?' I asked as soon as I'd said hello.

'She's securely locked up. She was arrested on the night of the 4th, last month,' Jussi said directly.

'Dear lord, why didn't you write and tell me?'

'Why would I? That's just the fashion in Leningrad these days. There's nothing unusual about that if you're a Finn. You just sit quietly and wait for your turn to come.'

'Tell me who,' I asked again, feeling short of breath.

In a measured voice, Jussi reeled off name after name. It seemed like the July heat was being drawn out of the room. I felt a chill and my mind was engulfed with sadness. Jussi just mechanically continued the roll call. When he'd finished, we stood in silence; there was nothing anyone could say that would make any difference.

But I couldn't get Oili out of my head. Did this spell the end for her? And all this time she'd been more worried about me than herself. How could she possibly endure this, already mentally numb, dragging her tired body around in there, in amongst the guards? I sifted through my recollections once again, remembering everything she had had to suffer within these Red walls. So much hurt, and now this as well. I recalled an evening in Leningrad, around twilight. It was just the two of us, and we were taking stock of everything we had experienced here up to then, filling in the blanks in each other's memories. A series of events floated past us like a short film that might well have been called '*Do You Remember?*'

But then Oili interjected: 'You know, Kaarina, you have a wonderful memory. You manage to keep everything so clear in your mind. I've often wished that you'll make it over the border some day. I mean, for heaven's sake, if you did it would be your duty to get it all written down – everything. Do you hear me, Kaarina? Everything! You could do it – it's well within your capability. At that point you'd having nothing to be afraid of and you could say everything openly and honestly.'

'You're completely mad! What else have you been dreaming about? Do you really think that the day will come when we get an opportunity here to do anything other than end up in a hole in the ground – and even that's probably more likely to happen in Siberia.'

'Well, that's just how it is, isn't it? Sometimes you go a little bit funny and start talking nonsense.'

We sat quietly. The room grew darker and darker, only the silhouettes of things were visible, and soon they, too, merged into blackness.

'I would give a lot just to know where we'll all eventually end up, where to look for his grave,' said Oili in a voice so dark it was as if it came from beneath the ground. I was shivering but not from cold. I said with bitterness, '"What you seek so shall you find", so the Russian proverb goes. I guess we found what we were looking for, Oili.'

Oili sprang up and made for the light switch on the wall. With a trembling voice she blurted out angrily, 'Oh my God! How stupid

– how insane can people be?! And there are still some people left in Finland who are crazy enough?'

The bright light flooded the room and released us for a moment from our nightmare vision of the future.

My dear Oili – wherever you are now – I hope the delicate vibrations in the realm of thought will transport my greetings to you. That impossible idea that you planted into my consciousness in that dark room: I have never stopped trying to turn it into reality for you, for Kari, for Aarno and for all my loved ones. I've let my pen fly free; I've revived my memories piece by piece; while still suffering, I have relived all that has passed to paint as full a picture as possible. And I did it simply because our insanity, as you called it, Oili, with your usual frankness and truthfulness, might warn other crazy people just like us about what kind of happiness awaited us under the five-pointed star in the land of the sickle and the sledgehammer. I like to think, my friend, that you would be pleased with what I've done.

27

Summer 1938

Jussi and Eero hadn't put much thought into it before they set off on their holiday trip. Neither of them had bothered to get a vacation certificate from their workplace, which I could have presented to the house commandant. Soviet law required every visitor staying for more than twenty-four hours to register and show their papers to the house commandant, who in turn reported the matter to the militia. Admittedly, it was difficult to keep on top of every single visitor, but in this period the commandants were very enthusiastic about following even the tiniest formality so as to keep themselves out of trouble. So, without certificates, I couldn't confirm the purpose of my guests' visit to Petrozavodsk, and so I swallowed hard and refrained from notifying the house commandant. Everything was going smoothly until Saturday night, when disaster struck.

Barani Bereg is a place on the opposite shore of Lake Onega, where the people of Petrozavodsk spent their summers in their small weekend chalets. On the day my guests chose to go there, I had an evening shift and couldn't accompany them, but Pirjo went, thanks to the neighbour who looked after her during my evening shifts. I didn't even bother going over to meet them on the Sunday.

That night, the NKVD carried out a mass inspection in Barani Bereg and gathered a large number of detainees. In the summer house, where Jussi, Eero and their hosts were staying, everyone showed their passports, including all three Leningradians: Jussi, Eero and a young man named Jaakkola. One by one the passports were checked and approved, until finally it was Jaakkola's turn. In the pages of his passport was a certificate issued in Leningrad.

'You're from Leningrad. Where's the posting? Or any other papers?'

Jaakkola tried to explain that they were holidaymakers there but had forgotten to get their vacation certificates before they set off, and that's why there weren't any papers. And besides they didn't think you really needed a certificate anyway.

'You're coming with us,' said one of the inspectors.

And that's when that fool Jaakkola decided to turn on Jussi and Eero: 'What about these other men here? They're on vacation from Leningrad and they don't have any papers either.'

'Oh, is that so? We hadn't noticed. Show me those papers again. Excellent. You two: come along as well. This matter will be resolved.'

The NKVD took them to the city to be grilled by the same machinery. After a couple of hours of intense interrogation, a paper was thrust in front of Jussi and Jaakkola, which contained an order to leave the city within twenty-four hours. Sign it and get out. But Eero remained in the NKVD building. Oili's son was a hard-working boy, eager to learn. Over the previous two winters, despite his poor Russian, he had been studying in the evenings after work, taking a ten-year course. He had a clear aim: study hard and become an electrical engineer (life had to get easier after that?). But these modest dreams were quashed inside the prison walls and finally extinguished for good by forced labour in some deportation camp or other; the Soviet sledgehammer crushed them, as it did the future hopes of countless others.

Jussi and Jaakkola shook the dust of Petrozavodsk off their feet at the first opportunity. They'd barely been back in Leningrad as free men for a month when the request came for them to go to the 'Big House', along Liteyny Avenue. This imposing NKVD building had been built mainly by Finnish defectors. It was rather ironic: having reached their dreamland and their freedom, their first task was to build the prison where so many of them would later spend their time.

Summer 1938

I think the Great Purge period was probably the hardest for many Karelian Finns. But I suppose I was already so numb that I didn't really react to it as strongly as I did to previous adversities. Of course, I was scared. Every night when I bolted the door shut I feared a nocturnal visit from the NKVD. I was afraid for my little darling; to be separated from her would have been the most gut-wrenching thing imaginable. In the evenings I watched my baby while she slept so I could etch that little face permanently onto my memory. 'What will come will come' was my motto.

I was absolutely convinced I wouldn't be spared. 'I'll be taken away,' I might say to myself a hundred times over. There was no hope of remaining free; for goodness sake — a widow like me! But, again, 'What will come will come'. If it was not the submission of the Supreme Will, the laying down of weapons of war, then I'd like to know what it was.

The factory administration seemed to share the opinion about how dangerous I was. I was moved from the side workshop to the main one, with such clear wording that no guesswork was needed. But I wasn't going to surrender as easily as that. My neighbour of many years was a lawyer and a member of the Karelia Supreme Court. I explained to this kind young Karelian how difficult it would be for me to carry on working and living with my child if I had to move out of the workshop next to Pirjo's nursery — where the lawyer's young wife also worked, and would help me on many occasions by taking my daughter there and bringing her back when I couldn't leave work. So I was given a long official letter to hand to the administration — a letter in which my neighbour expressed his puzzlement about the administration's attitude towards a lonely mother, a worker for many years, whose life was being impeded by this decision, despite the fact the woman was already in need of assistance; in passing he also mentioned the service his wife undertook for my child. He signed the letter with his name and his title in bold pen strokes, underneath which he specified a location where he could be met should more information be required. The outcome was excellent: I got to stay in the side workshop; I seemed to have a powerful protector on my side.

For a while, everything went well. On 16 July 1938, the director of the workshop approached me and showed me a finding of the People's Court regarding something I didn't understand; right then, the manager informed me that a car was coming to pick me up outside the factory. I was quite taken aback, of course, but I soon understood it for what it must surely be. In my mind, I was saying farewell to the whole world, and, tearlessly, I cried for my little Pirjo, who might never see her mother again.

Outside, there was indeed a car waiting for me, but not a single NKVD man to be seen, only our apartment building commandant. I tried to explain that I didn't have my passport with me and that I wanted to run to the nursery to say goodbye to my daughter, but the house commandant just kept repeating some jargon or other, which I didn't understand. It was something about moving, changing apartments, or at least something along those lines. I climbed into the car and a faint hope began to dawn.

The car was actually heading to my home, and there in the yard I saw seven or eight men, none of whom, to my joy, were NKVD. A deep sigh of relief escaped my chest. Thanks to one of my neighbours acting as interpreter, the whole thing finally came to light.

I had already been subjected twice before to civil court hearings on account of my apartment. They wanted to evict me on the grounds that the house no longer belonged to the city's municipal department, and it was from them that I had previously obtained permission to move. On both occasions, the court had been lenient. As I had a young child, I was allowed to continue living there until my workplace, the city council, or the new owner of the building, the company Karelstroi, who might require it for their own workers, provided me and my child with a suitable apartment. So long as none of these bodies was able to do this for me, I got to keep my former room. But now, as a result of numerous imprisonments, homes had been vacated and that's what had led to this sudden commotion about relocation.

'If you don't move now,' continued my neighbour the interpreter, 'then next time it could mean eviction to somewhere outside the city.'

Summer 1938

So what else could I do? I let these eight men pick all my stuff up, shove it randomly in and on top of the vehicle, sit on top of the pile and leave. I comforted myself with the thought that at least it wasn't a trip to the jail.

My new apartment was bigger and better. By the time I'd got all my possessions unpacked and arranged, I really couldn't have been more pleased.

I still had time to pop into work, where they were amazed by my resurrection. They must have had enough time to mourn my fate, because all their faces were beaming with genuine relief and goodwill.

It was only a few days after this incident that the deportations of the families of imprisoned people began all over the city. On the first night, with no advance warning, people were rudely awakened and ordered to collect their belongings. Both NKVD and militia men pitched in to help get the items out of the houses. Party members were also found to be quite helpful, among all the hustle and bustle.[24] It was hard to bear the crying of the children, the grief of the women and to see the men being so miserable and quiet. Cars queued up on the dock to unload, only to turn around to pick up another family with their belongings. The great barges moored to the pier absorbed all these people and their property; in the morning, off they went, lazily towed by steamboats with their inconsolable payload. The first night's catch was taken to remote Olenia Island, which had a quarry, a limestone trench and an incinerator.

That first night was followed by others, but before long some kind of a system had been imposed. Now you were notified a day and a half in advance, good citizens, that you needed to pack your goods, so they could be removed more efficiently. The second batch was also transported by barge, but this time to Pudozh, a well-known deportee destination, where they could all apply to the locals for an apartment and hope they were one of the lucky ones.

On the third night, the escorts formed a solid ring around the deportees. Both those inside the ring and the escorts responded to

---

24 These were not acts of altruism alone. Vacant apartments meant opportunities for 'upgrades'.

the situation with gallows humour. Many were drunk, but cautious not to annoy the officials, the NKVD men. One crumb of comfort was the unexpected update that infants and pregnant women were no longer forced to participate in this journey, although they had been on the previous two occasions.

The third group was taken to Shyoltozero, where they were deposited mainly in forest locations. All of them had at least one family member imprisoned, but no passports were taken from them, even after this deportation. Thus, as citizens, theirs was just a short compulsory transfer away from the capital of the republic to a less populated area.

The deportations created more vacant housing in the city, but it was still not enough. More was needed for NKVD soldiers and staff and for the militia.[25] And more was indeed obtained, thanks to new coercive measures.

The most heartbreaking example of the officials' disregard for people's age or any other considerations was the expulsion of my old friend whom I called Aunt Maija. Maija was an old worker from Vyborg who, from a very young age, had dedicated her life to the cause. For decades she had worked, unpaid, in a life of self-sacrifice for what she thought was right. For almost nine full years, she had languished in the Hämeenlinna Women's Prison in Finland, proud to endure her time there because she thought she was doing it for the cause. When she was finally released from prison, at almost 50 years of age, she left for Russia, more to do the will of others than her own. Of course, she was well received. She ended up as a matron in a Karelian rest home and never held back in praising Rovio and Gylling for their modesty and kindness while they were staying as guests. Even under Irklis she kept her position, but now life in the rest home was very different. Irklis demanded theatricality and luxury. Aunt Maija could not cope with this new ethos and resigned.

Despite being in the autumn of her life, she married and lived a quiet life with her husband, having taken a job in Petrozavodsk.

---

25 This is a possible reference to preparations for potential escalation in Europe.

Oddly enough, she had been spared imprisonment, although her husband, a quiet forest worker who had never got involved in any public activities, was thrown in jail that spring. A few days after his arrest, Aunt Maija found her door sealed. For that she could thank the house commandant who did it while she was at work; he had been heard to say while he was locking down her dwelling, 'Let her find somewhere else to live: she'll be in prison soon enough anyway.'

Maija's door was released later that same day after she had run around to various places, only to be locked down again the following day while she was at work. And so an old woman in her 60s, in spite of all her dedication to the workers' cause, was left totally abandoned in the street in nothing but a thin work blouse.

She spoke to me in tears: 'And so this finally happened to me as well – my reward for all I've done.'

'Come and stay with us, Aunt Maija,' I implored, my eyes also filled with tears.

'Thank you, but I've already agreed to stay somewhere else. At least I have friends, so I don't have to stay out on the street like the government wants me to. I'll try to see the Republican procurator tomorrow and see if I can get that door open so I can at least pick up my clothes.'

She did in fact get her door released. But this old weary woman was part of the third deportation wave and taken to the Shyoltozero district for logging and felling duties.

Autumn 1938

By the look of things, not enough homes had been vacated as a result of these arrests and deportations, and that obstinate Finnish population had not been sufficiently thinned out. New forms would have to be issued – a bit less severe, but still harsh enough.

'Kaarina, have you received an order to go to Andreiev, the head of the militia?' was what I was greeted with one morning in autumn 1938.

'No. Why?'

My co-workers explained. Several Finnish families in Petrozavodsk had been invited to appear before Andreiev in the next couple of days, where their deportation order would be issued: leave the city at their own expense within a certain timeframe. This fate fell particularly on the heads of residents of the former cooperative houses built by American Finns, and on those of the former cooperative house called 'Builder', built mainly by Finns. One day in early winter, these houses were forcibly taken away from the cooperatives: a nominal amount was paid to the residents and they were declared the property of the city municipal department. Although the residents were allowed to remain as tenants, any unneeded space had to be rented out to others. These groups of houses were jolly-looking places, in stark contrast to the general grey. The Finnish supervisory boards had kept the houses in good condition, and, despite some deterioration owing to several years of neglect by the municipal department, they were still an object of envy and desire for the official establishment, mainly because they were inhabited by Finns. No new houses like these had been built since; anything new that sprang up could not compare in quality to these so-called 'American barracks'.

So now Andreiev, the head of the militia, took advantage of Matushenko's orders to kill two birds with one stone: not only could he get rid of the Finns by spreading them far and wide across Russia but he could free up some apartments at the same time.

All my colleagues had been ordered to appear before Andreiev at noon that day. That morning, not much work got done; everyone was weighing up their chances of whether they would be allowed to stay or, if not, where they could go. They were all American Finns and elderly.

'Kaarina, sing a song for us again. Sing "Homeland",' someone asked me. I was in the habit of singing to myself in the middle of work when the opportunity arose. So I sang. I sang that Soviet citizens' song about the homeland. I let the notes rise higher, higher, as if to mock this great freedom that all my comrades around me knew only too well:

> Broad is my dear country,
> Covered over with forests, rivers and fields.
> I know of no other land
> where anyone could be so free.[26]

'Oh, that's so true!' everyone agreed once I'd got to the end of the chorus. They all said it at the same time, raising their heads with a deep sigh. Life in Finland and America was called to mind: countries where you had a very different kind of freedom. The Soviet citizen will sing his song not really knowing anything about the truly free countries, but for my listeners songs of freedom were not new. Yes, people were 'free' here, but the devil take this 'freedom'!

---

26 This English translation is the editor's.

Autumn 1938

'Andreiev is made out of stone,' said my old colleague that evening. He continued, 'I told him – as well I might – that it's just not fair for a person like me, at the age of 60, to be told to get out of the apartment and move out of town. I've worked all my life; I've never broken the law and I've done no wrong. I asked him if he could let the matter drop. So Andreiev nodded, agreed with me, but stuck to his decision anyway. And I've no idea where I'm supposed to go.'

No one else could understand it either, but before long family after family were travelling obediently without knowing what awaited them at their destination. Many sold their small houses on the outskirts of the city for nothing more than bank credit, at a fraction of the price they'd bought them for. And so the Finns were scattered far and wide, quietly and with bitterness.

Many Finns of their own volition put themselves forward to go deeper into the forest or some outpost in Russia in order to avoid arrest or deportation. Such acts of volunteering might come off, but then again they might not, because the imprisonments weren't just happening in the cities but wherever Finns and Karelians were living; Karelians, too, were taken away in large numbers – whole villages would be completely emptied or have no men left in them.

I often wondered where all those prisoners must have ended up. They started their journeys from the 'White House' in Petrozavodsk or the 'Big House' in Leningrad, but where they went after that ... who knows? Gradually, information began to be uncovered that could shed some light. Appalling stories about the 'Red Terror' began to circulate, though hardly anyone dared to repeat them except in a whisper. It was a desperate thing to hear the terrible fate of loved ones.

In Kivimäki, near Petrozavodsk, right on the outskirts of the city, there was a lonely barracks, from which the quiet summer nights were rent with terrifying cries of pain. Those who managed to find their way out of the barracks were able to confirm that the rumours were true: through whips and torture, innocent people were being blackmailed into signing falsified interrogation statements.

An American Finn, who was elderly and disabled, spoke in horror of how he had been beaten and ordered to stand still until he fainted.

The screaming of those being tortured came constantly from the other rooms.

'Write down what the hell you want: just stop hitting me!' he had told his tormentors in pain.

Another, who had once served in Ekenäs prison camp,[27] spoke with disgust about some Finnish men who had agreed to act as so-called 'whips' to save their own skin. Can there be any lousier individual than a coward like that?! This was the same person who some time ago had been sent to Crimea, having come to Russia to recover from the trauma of a Finnish prison. As fate would have it, he later found himself being sent on another 'journey of rest', this time in even greater need of recovery. He had been convicted once again – by the Soviets this time. However, in a more favourable season, during the reign of the Terijoki People's Government, he was considered useful again, given a party membership card and a free trip to a Crimean rest home to heal his Soviet prison injuries. Spiritually and physically battered, he let them do what they wanted there, but no amount of head stroking could resurrect that fiery 100 per cent revolutionary soul.

There was another hellish prison camp in Kondopoga. The stories from there were so horrific that they do not bear repeating, but are best forgotten.

There was a young girl, who was born in the country, and I recall her once trying to find some mitigating circumstances when we were talking about torture: 'That's just down to individual viciousness. You can't blame the Soviet system for that: it's those savages who've let a lust for power go to their heads.'

'But how can you explain how all of this can happen? Just think about it for a minute: the administration of an entire prison camp is getting its staff to torture people under investigation.'

---

27 The prison camp in Ekenäs was originally supposed to be a temporary fixture but it ended up serving as a prison for twenty years. It mainly housed the 'Reds' – the side that lost the Civil War in Finland. At least 3,000 people died here owing to poor hygiene, lack of food and disease.

'Oh, don't ask me: I don't know. I just need to believe that people higher up won't allow it to happen or else they don't know anything about it. I'll go crazy if I have to think about it too much.'

So there it was again: the straitjacket around the mind. This young Soviet girl had to suppress her thoughts about such questions — she just wanted to believe.

Of course, there were quite a few who were released and claimed that nothing had happened to them. That might have been true for some, but how many mouths were kept closed by intimidation? I know so many of them — I've heard more than I would ever care to — but I've promised most of them to forget about it and let their horror stories remain unspoken.

It was often the case that a prisoner could no longer be found in the area indicated in their papers or in any of the prison camps. So it was with the daughter-in-law of the famous Kuusinen.[28] Kuusinen managed to get his son released but his daughter-in-law could not be traced and probably remains unaccounted for to this day. The NKVD papers will keep her hidden forever somewhere in an unknown corner of the vastness of Russia.

Everyone remembers what a fuss the disappearance of the lawyer Asser Salo[29] once caused in Finland. He was imprisoned in Petrozavodsk in 1937. The men of the Karelian–Finnish Republic tried to get him released with petitions and requests to have him appointed as some sort of professor of law at the University of Petrozavodsk — a fruitless effort as it turned out. Asser Salo was never seen again.

The wave of Great Purge took away much of the Finnish working--class left-wing base, which the Motherland's extreme Soviet supporters declared to be for the best. These men and women were tried and true, the most capable, the most ideal. But they fell short in

---

28 Otto Wille Kuusinen was a Finnish politician who headed the puppet government in late 1939. He could not return to Finland after the war and remained loyal to the Communist Party. (He is the only Finn ever to be buried within the Kremlin wall.)
29 A former member of the Finnish Parliament. He was imprisoned and shot in 1938.

the judgement of the Red homeland, so much so that they were not fit for anything other than Siberia, as residents of the Komi region or some other remote area. And that's where they went, with guards right and left, in front and behind.

29

Late 1938 to Late 1939

With the Great Purge at its most frantic pitch and amidst all those mass deportations, I entered into another marriage. It was more straightforward and simpler this time. As the Great Purge raged on, I was feeling desperately lonely night after night as I awaited my arrest. To be sure, I was completely prepared for it and very much expecting it, acquiescent and miserable, as if facing something predetermined and inescapable.

My continued freedom was a surprise to everyone, and most people had something to say about it: 'It's a miracle that you haven't been taken away yet, Kaarina – a two-times prison widow! Many poor souls end up there for nothing, and yet you ... I just don't get it.'

To be honest, that kind of thing wasn't exactly fun to listen to. But no malice was intended and it didn't offend me. I mean, it's not as if I wasn't having the exact same thought: it preyed on my mind day and night. For heaven's sake, though, prison was surely all I could look forward to. What could possibly save me from Siberia?

But then an old acquaintance from years ago, Martti Varpio, took me completely by surprise by asking me, in the most matter-of-fact way, to marry him: 'You need to change your name. And I believe I have a bachelor's surname that's not linked to any prisons. The only work done under this name has been hard manual work. And, if we have to, we can travel around Russia, just like all the other Finns. I mean, anyway, as a man, I've got more chance of keeping your girl from starving than a woman on your own like you.'

That was true. All the same, I tried to explain what a dubious dowry I would be bringing into our household. How many men have been deported after their wife was imprisoned, yet here I am ...

'Forget it: I know all about it. I don't have a party membership card to lose or a commander's rank. And I can get work anywhere.'

I still don't understand why this bachelor would take such a risk and marry a widow like me at that time. It felt like a bad joke.

Martti had first arrived here as a recruit from Canada.

'I was unemployed for a year and a half. The Comintern[30] newspapers were blaring out in every country about how the current world crisis was terminal, irrevocable. So, because I had time on my hands, I thought it would be a good idea to go to Russia to help build a model for socialism.'

That was how he, half-jokingly among friends, described how he ended up in Russia.

With Martti, things took a significant turn for the better financially as he earned a good wage at a nearby lumberyard. He was a practical man by nature, caring and considerate. And I was now free from money worries, perhaps for the first time. Besides, Pirjo was happy to have a father. She started bringing her little friends from the neighbourhood over just to show him off. For ages she'd been asking me to 'buy me a proper daddy'.

Perhaps it was the change of name and the sudden change of address that threw the authorities off the scent in the midst of all the chaos of the Great Purge, and that's what spared me from the dungeon. By the autumn, life in every way was feeling calmer.

Matushenko, the most cursed man in Karelia, suffered the same fate as his predecessor. The Russians said they had read in the papers that

---

30 The Comintern (also known as the Communist International, and also known as the Third International) was an organisation that advocated internationally for communism.

his days had come to an end by order of the same institution in which he had been acting as a ruthless whip. His legacy was truly appalling. However, none of the expected corrective measures were taken. Only a few people were released from prison. The Puutos, Oleny Island and Lake Shyoltozero deportees were permitted to return to the city as long as their applications proved they had found an apartment, either through their workplace or through private individuals. It was the only restitution of any significance and the only gesture made.

★ ★ ★

As 1939 rolled in, new laws came into force regarding absences from work and the reduction of women's maternity leave. The mass transfer of the labour force to Siberia had left significant shortages everywhere else. Yet there was an increasing amount of work to be done. So they tried whatever they could to intensify the working day. The new law required managers to dismiss anyone who was more than twenty minutes late on any single occasion – or late at all more than twice. These dismissals were legal matters under a decision of the People's Court. Initially, the law stipulated that a person dismissed in this way could not be offered another job for six months, but this was quickly relaxed so you could walk into a new job the following day. So a law that began by being punitive ended up being very useful if you wanted to change jobs or poach professionals from other institutions – things that were previously impossible. All you had to do was turn up late, so management had to dismiss you, and you were free to go elsewhere.

But the reduction of maternity leave was another story. Going back to the Lenin era, the law had exempted pregnant women from work, with two months' leave of absence on full pay both before and after giving birth. Now – ostensibly at women's own request – this leave was reduced by almost half: to thirty-five days before giving birth and only twenty-eight days after. Women were clearly not happy about this, of course, but, having got used to putting up with all the other laws they'd been subjected to, they yielded to this as well.

Before summer was over, we noticed goods in shops gradually disappearing from the shelves. There were queues for certain groceries, amounts were being rationed, and you could wait for hours for some goods to turn up. Cheap items, like salted cod and vegetable oil, were so scarce that hundreds of people were queuing up all night to buy them. These shortages got people thinking about the likely reason behind them. In all likelihood, it was because we were preparing for war, even though the *politruks*[31] sending out the messages had been insisting for years that, if war did break out, the country would be drowned in food and other goods. In such a situation, they argued, all goods produced would have to be consumed within our own borders. Lack of goods in the past had been blamed on exports, with produce being sold to buy machines from abroad to supply Soviet industry.

On 7 September 1939, we got our answer. The Polish War began. Or, to be more precise, that's when men in Karelia were mobilised, albeit only the Russians this time. Some ordinary people knew what was happening: the throngs of women hanging miserably around the barrack gates for hours on end just to see a glimpse of their husbands and sons.

The Polish War was a strange one and gave us much to think about. It was the agreement between Germany and the Soviet Union that was the real shock. We had always been taught to regard Germany as the greatest enemy of the Soviet land. Newspapers and pamphlets had been relentlessly stirring up hatred towards Germany, and we'd had films showing us how much misery, hunger, imprisonment and death Germany had visited on its own country. Basically, anti-German propaganda had been as brutal and intense as you could imagine. Now there was a complete turnaround. The magazines wrote elegies to Germany's virtue and beauty, anti-German films disappeared, and political actors on all sides came forward to heap praise on the country. No one mentioned German misery any more, or its rigid systems, or the rationing. Although by now you had got used to all

---

31 A *politruk* was the name given to a political officer in the Communist countries.

manner of twists and turns in government policy, this somersault beggared all belief.

The conscription of Russians into the ranks gave us no reason to suspect that Finnish men would be eligible as well. But how little we knew.

On 17 November, I was walking home on my own, thinking about my Pirjo, because I'd just come back from taking her to the ear hospital for treatment. At the corner of Komsomolskaya and Marx Street, I almost ran straight into Martti.

'Well, my darling, it looks like I'm off to war. The Military Advisory Agency has sent me the order. Apparently, we Finns are still valid citizens!'

Martti was laughing and trying to downplay how serious it was by joking about it.

'Oh God, that's all we need! You won't be going there straight away?'

'I don't think I'll be leaving in these clothes. They'll probably give me a check-up first. I'll at least go and change into my worst clothes so it doesn't matter when they get thrown into storage and lost. So there you go: maybe I will be wearing the Crown's garments after all. Although I doubt they'll dare to use us for anything more than digging ditches, all these ex-convicts.'

Martti was always like that: joking around, even in the direst situations, and especially if he thought I was getting anxious. Such banter was just what I had to expect in situations like this. It was the same gallows humour that would have me as 'the widow of the would-be generals', as he sometimes referred to me. So now I couldn't help but worry as I continued my journey home.

It was after midnight when Martti finally came home.

'Every single Finnish man in Petrozavodsk and the surrounding area has been called up and nearly all of them have been selected.'

'Were there a lot of familiar faces?'

'Well, of course, considering any man under 55 who looks Finnish or Karelian was there. Some had already brought their wives with them.'

'So where are they taking you?'

'Well, they weren't divulging any state secrets. It'll be for excavation work, of course: how do you think we'll get on, working on the sidelines? Dirty and covered with lice doing that kind of job, I expect. What do you reckon?'

'I reckon you're impossible! Now be serious for a minute. What did the interrogators say to you?'

'Do I think I can cope with the local language. And have I ever served any time in the military. I said I was a bit so-so as far as the language was concerned, but I learned all the basic soldiering drill commands in Vähäheikkilä in Turku and I can still do them without thinking about it. That's no lie, either. Would you like me to show you, darling?'

'No, you don't need to do that! What else did they ask you?'

'Only about my brothers, and I said there were four more like me living by the river in Kokemäki, each of them about 6ft tall. The bigger commander laughed and said it was all good. Told me to shear all the wool off and come back to the same place with a mug and a spoon at 1 p.m. on Monday. Please don't ask me anything else, Kaarina.'

On Monday, I escorted Martti to Enlightenment House,[32] which was as busy as an anthill, bustling with Finnish and Karelian men. There didn't seem to be many commanders there, but the few that were there all looked very distinguished. Throughout the day and the day before, cars had been bringing men in from the surrounding area: Kondopoga, Shuya, Matrosy and so on. I couldn't for the life of me work out why Ingrians or even the Leningrad Finns were being brought to Petrozavodsk.

All the escorts were expelled into the outer foyer on the other side of some large glass doors. The men inside in the hall were divided into two groups: shorn and unshorn. I'd only just scissored Martti's locks that morning and, being tall, he stuck out among those on his

---

[32] The base for Kansanvalistusseura, the Finnish Lifelong Learning Foundation.

side of the room. The long-haired got what was coming to them: failing to cut their hair was taken as a deliberate act of neglect and disregard for military standards. One Karelian spoke in Russian to the Russian commander saying that he hadn't had any money to pay the barber. The commander fixed him with a look and said irately, 'But you received your final pay!'

'Well, everything happened in such a rush, and my family needs all that money,' the man objected, bravely.

The commander was livid: 'You should have informed me about that at the enrolment centre. A small amount like that – anyone would have given it to you. Not an acceptable defence!' He continued sternly: 'Everyone else can go and get their hair cut. But you!' – he turned to the Karelian – 'You leave your name and personal information with me. We will discuss this later somewhere else.'

It was a clear warning to the others: think about it before you open your mouth.

The company of Finns was a serious-looking bunch. Some of them seemed a bit scared, their eyes glancing from one to another as they sought some explanation for what was going on. Some 100 per centers were beaming, but most faces betrayed a depression born of capitulation. Only a year ago, Finnishness had been trampled into the dust and three times cursed; it had been constantly battered and abused. And now what? It had become eligible for active service! There were some among these people who, with the help of vodka, were celebrating this unexpected 'promotion'.

The men were transferred to various barracks – mainly the large stone-built one on Uritski Street near my workplace. For several days I was able to talk to Martti through the gaps in the fence; but he wasn't able to get a sense of what on earth was going on in there.

'I think they're working on getting some kind of army of the Finnish tribes together,' he said. 'I just sat quietly on the side when they were picking men for the different specialties. I decided to let them worry about it. I didn't bother telling them I'd been a signaller in the Finnish Army. In the end, they put me in the transport corps. Let's see when the uniforms arrive.'

We didn't have to wait very long as it turned out. That same night, wearing his brand-new green People's Army overcoat, my warrior popped home. He grimaced as he spun round showing off his fine array: 'I look pretty flash now, don't I?'

'Any ideas about where you're going to?' I asked, stroking the fine green fabric.

'Not a chance! Not even when we set off.'

All of a sudden, next morning, off they went. They were stationed near Leningrad in Detskoye Selo.

30

November 1939

Everywhere the following week there was talk of Finland's attack on the Soviet Union. Is that what those close negotiations between Molotov[33] and the Finnish representatives were all about? I wondered how likely it actually was that an invading side would be entering such negotiations. However, with all the news being about the Shelling of Mainila,[34] you were required to believe – sheer impossibility though it was – that the Finnish administration were so stupid that they were unable to comprehend what attacking a superpower might lead to.

At work, we had a *miitinki* – an on-the-job meeting in which a *politruk* spoke to us in Russian to explain the Mainila situation and Molotov's speech. He claimed that attempt after attempt had been made to steer the Finnish Government towards peace, but they – allegedly – were intransigent. Finland apparently forgot that it had the Soviet Union to thank for its independence. If, however, Finland felt that it was so well prepared that it need not fear the consequences, then it would have to face what was coming to it alone. This was

---

33 A leading figure in the Soviet Government from the 1920s onwards.
34 The Shelling of Mainila is the name given to an incident on 26 November 1939, in which the Soviet Union claimed unfriendly fire from Finland had caused loss of life on the Soviet side of the border. Historians (on all sides) are unanimous in their opinion that the story was fabricated by the NKVD in order to justify declaring war.

followed by a long diatribe praising the Red Army, for anyone who was still listening. He also said something about Finland's magnificent concrete-built 'Mannerheim Line' cutting off all Karelia entirely, about its iron defence capabilities, and about how it was to be used as a central base in plans to attack Leningrad. The *politruk* ended his speech with a plea to everyone's sense of justice: everyone is entitled to their opinion, of course – but are we to allow the borders of the Soviet Union to be violated in this way?

His language was more colourful than that, but that was the gist. A few comments followed. The pedigree and views of the commentators were already well known. When anything fresh was being pushed on us, it was customary to invite some 'reliable' workers to the manager's private room before the meeting started. They were instructed about what to support. So the comments just lent weight to the meeting's agenda, even if the occasional daredevil spoke up to offer a mild difference of opinion. So, with the customary help of the planted assistants, we heard about the 'rabid Finnish instigators of war' who required 'a punch in the face', and the meeting was seen to give Molotov its blessing. The same slogans about 'pig snouts' and so on were revisited, having been regurgitated for years by orators, magazines and radio stations.

And what about those Finns whose lives had begun over the border, who had been brought up there, or had even lived there as adults? Could we really be at war with that country? At first it just seemed impossible. With mounting horror, I did a mental calculation of the distance between where my relatives lived and the border area.

Meanwhile, the bitterness just got worse. Did the Finnish Government really not realise the danger that a war posed to the country's independence and its democracy? The Red Army could potentially call up enough men to outnumber all of Finland's small population. The Red Army had never had to go cap in hand to acquire funding: it was given everything – down to the latest motorised armoured vehicles, as well as all the supplies it needed, even while the people were starving. No, and a thousand times no: Finland should not be going to war, at least not as the aggressors. I saw no other

November 1939

outcome for Finland than ending up as part of this people's prison, probably sporting a name like 'Soviet Finland'. There had been a time many years ago when a name like that, written in letters of fire, had flown high in the sky of my dreams. That was one daydream that I paid a hefty price for, seeing as I hadn't managed to see this insanity for what it was before the payment was due. Now the thought of 'Soviet Finland' filled me with horror.

On 3 December, there was another rumble in the factory. The radio announced – in Finnish, no less – that Terijoki[35] had been captured and that the Finns had declared their own democratic government, with Otto Wille Kuusinen as prime minister, Akseli Anttila as minister of war, Tuure Lehén as minister of the interior, Inkeri Lehtinen as minister of education – and so on and so on.

'Hey, Kaarina, are you sleepwalking even with all this noise going on around you? In a week or so you'll be seeing your son in Helsinki,' exclaimed my exhilarated foreman, a former Finnish newspaper man who had miraculously avoided prison during the Great Purge by infiltrating himself into his old profession behind the tailor's table. As far as he was concerned, all this commotion simply meant advancement – which is why he was so excited and slapped me on my back so hard that it hurt.

Yes – that's what it had finally come to. After all those years of separation, I was really going to see my Poju again. My dream would come true: Poju and Pirjo together at the same time, side by side. I would have given so much to see that vision realised. But at what price?! 'Soviet Finland.' A price that was so high it made me feel sick. 'Soviet Finland!' That's where this was heading. And it would become reality at the sharp end of the Red Army bayonets. My mind kept forming pictures of what would be happening in Finland from now on. But I was too well accustomed to the discipline in this country to betray the slightest impression of how horrified I truly was. So I just sat and watched the noisy crowd. All at once, hot tears welled up in my eyes. I blinked, trying to hold them back. My throat choked with a silent pain. I would settle for losing

---

35 Now known as Zelenogorsk.

all hope of seeing my beloved Poju again, or my beautiful old mother – and who doesn't think their own mother is beautiful? – or my devoted father; I would trade all that in rather than see a 'Soviet Finland'. These thoughts rose up from my heart like a last prayer before drowning. I was willing to sacrifice my future life, all my hazy hopes and dreams, if it would guarantee lasting happiness for Poju, for my parents, for the people of my little homeland.

Our manager walked past me and noticed my tears. He grabbed me firmly by my shoulders, shook them violently with both hands and said delightedly, 'Yes, Kaarina Karlovna! I know why you're crying. That's right! Tears of joy for the future of little Finland. Now it really will become great: the Soviet Union will control it and it can develop without being hampered any more by money and the capitalist system.'

'And it won't take long, either. The 6th of this month is Finland's old Independence Day. Maybe the red flag will already be flying by then in Helsinki. In any case, it won't take more than two weeks.' This was my brigadier speaking so solemnly.

'And then you won't be doing this kind of work any more,' someone said to him. 'You'll be a big player soon, no doubt.'

'Let's just get on with our lives, boys, and we'll see, shall we?' the foreman replied, in a show of modesty. Turning to me, he continued, 'You're becoming very sombre. You take everything so seriously, Kaarina. If anyone needs to be putting a trip to Helsinki in their diary, it's you.'

'Oh, and what joy would that be,' I said to myself. Trying to hide what I was really thinking, I attempted a brisk tone of voice and a little laugh, saying, 'You'd be bawling your eyes out, too, if you'd just found out you were going to see your son after all these years.'

'Of course, yes. I remember how crazy you were when you came here without him. You should have brought him with you.'

How awful would that have been, I thought. Poju has been having a bright and happy childhood; he's certainly not missing out on anything. At least not up until now, even if we do have to share all this greyness together from now on.

November 1939

Martti was able to send messages every now and then with news about himself. He told me about his travels. They really had been at the receiving end of the Russian organisational machine. First of all, the Finns had been hauled from Leningrad and the surrounding area to Petrozavodsk, then taken back to Leningrad, then to the shores of the Arctic Ocean in Murmansk and Petsamo. The People's Army was, after all, just for show. Some of it was sent to the Terijoki Government to show support; and small sections had been sent to different border areas, but most to Petsamo. As soon as the Red Army had reached Helsinki, the various People's Army units would have rushed to the Finnish capital to march in a parade. The world had to get the impression that the People's Army was something that had sprung up voluntarily within Finland's borders – and in no way a Soviet fabrication.

But little Finland did not surrender within two weeks. Nor within a month. The radio didn't give much away, though. All the radio sets had been confiscated anyway and stored in government warehouses on the pretext that they were interfering with aircraft radio communications. Radio broadcasts in Finnish were now coming in every day, which could be listened to via point radio. In every possible way, 'Finnishness' was being promoted again. Many got their party membership cards back, and courses were being established because 'Soviet Finland' needed its national officials.

'Oh, I'm going to need so many workers for Finland,' said Karelia's minister of affairs, Comrade Prokkonen. 'I'll be damned! I'll need police chiefs, bailiffs, clerks and all the rest,' he added with a laugh.

Finns were advised not to delay in submitting their applications for entry into Finland. I didn't bother submitting mine, but no one ever seemed to get any result from an application anyway.

The small Finnish Army was putting up a massive resistance to the might of the Red Army. It was quite incredible. Time alone brought the facts home to us, because the press wasn't divulging a thing.

31

Winter 1939

The war dragged on. My point radio couldn't tell me much after the capture of Terijoki – apart from the fact that the fighting was fierce, but this much I knew anyway.

Near my apartment stood a large military hospital, only just built that same year, which had started to receive the wounded. As we walked past it after our evening shift, we could see the transport trucks lining up to unload their woeful cargoes, carefully and silently, at the side door. At first we shrank away from the sight, but we soon got so used to it that we barely noticed it in passing. Later, you could see soldiers with hypothermia being brought in at all times of the day.

In mid-December, the youth work organiser at our workplace began recruiting volunteers for blood donations. He went on at great length, stressing how grateful the Red Army was to every 'volunteer' donor. You didn't dare not put your name down, even if it wasn't technically mandatory.

At the Medical Commission check-up, I was given a clean bill of health and pronounced fit to donate blood. Although I was very pleased with the diagnosis, I was hesitant all the same. I recalled how back in Finland my mother used to run round making sure I got enough vitamins inside me because she worried about my anaemia. The most disgusting thing she used to give me was raw liver grated on top of a slice of bread. I put aside my misgivings when an invitation to donate arrived from the State Blood Transfusion Committee. We formed a large crowd as we climbed the Petrozavodsk Surgical Hospital stairs that morning.

The hospital was the old type from the days of imperial rule, and we had these in Finland, too: a three-storey building with very high ceilings and extraordinarily long corridors. Now, all you could see everywhere were wounded men. There were beds pushed up against each other in the hallways, leaving just a narrow alley to walk down between the ends of the beds, so narrow that it was almost single-file. Wailing came from all sides with some occasional shouting. The wards themselves were also full to bursting, as we could plainly see through the open doors. It made me feel nauseous, this human repair shop, with its seemingly endless corridors.

My young Karelian colleagues wandered around curiously, wearing the white coats we had all been given, and reported back to me that the hospital was indeed crammed full of wounded men.

'They're everywhere!'

The queue of donors outside the operating theatre didn't seem to be moving at all to begin with. A constant stream of young soldiers were being carried in while unconscious ones were being carried out. The hospital staff hurried busily back and forth.

All of us in our white coats, we went looking on all the various floors for some toilets. Well, we did find some, but I almost died of repulsion when I saw them. The toilets were full to the brim, overflowing onto the floor, going everywhere in stinking waves. Some bright spark had simply placed a wide wooden board across the doorstep all the way from one side to the other, and the staff on either side just carried on as if everything was normal. What an awful sight in a big hospital like this! Although I'd seen toilets just as bad in other places in Russia. I was shaken and disgusted. But the hospital sisters were relaxed about it: 'It's because of the frost: the pipes froze – what can you do about it?!'

Were they just calmly waiting until spring for all that sludge to start moving of its own accord?

Finally, it was my turn to go in. In the anteroom another quick check, a blood sample from my fingertip, and then told to lie down on a small table in the larger room. With my arm resting on a stand, a masked female doctor began her work. I lay quietly and looked around, taking in what I could. In the middle of the floor, under a large suspended mirror, lay a soldier on an operating table, his stomach open. Three masked doctors were at work around him, nurses standing by with bandages and surgical instruments on trays. The door was constantly opening and closing as the other staff moved about. To my surprise, a man in a black civilian suit walked up to the patient and spoke vehemently to the doctor. They weren't even left in peace to operate.

'All right, up you get. 350g. Feel dizzy?'

I was unsteady, but I think it was mostly from hunger. I had last eaten the night before; this morning I'd been in a rush to get here and hadn't had anything more than a cup of tea. Now it was 4.30 p.m., apparently. I'd spent my whole day in this hospital.

But they'd put on a good dinner for us downstairs: strong meat soup, mashed potatoes with sausages and gravy, and, to finish off, apricot custard. The cashier paid 50 roubles per 100g, so I got 175 roubles.

A couple of days later I became ill. Perhaps it was down to my cold apartment: I had a cold and both my lungs were inflamed. Perhaps it was also something to do with donating too much blood at the wrong time. I was ill for a month and it was only thanks to Aunt Maija's diligent care that I finally got out of bed. The few friends I had all did their best, each of them bringing me something to eat or some milk, which often involved a lot of effort for them and long queues.

Indeed, access to food, which was already well-nigh impossible, only worsened as the war went on. Queuing all day didn't get you anywhere now: you had to queue all night just to get something to eat. Families of the regular army, the NKVD and the militia, however, could usually get all their supplies from their own closed shops; but you couldn't use them if you didn't have a card. How often did I run directly from work at 11 p.m. at the end of my evening shift, straight to the nearest shop to join a queue that had already started to form at 7 p.m.? I'd spend all night there shivering, despite the fatigue, and when the door opened at 11 a.m., I'd be happy with anything they still had left for me. Then I'd stagger like a zombie home, where little Pirjo had been waiting all alone – although sometimes the old lady next door would glance over to see if she was all right – wolf down some hot concoction or other and then head out again, if it was a day off, to the market hall just in case I was able to find something else before night came round again. Now that's what you call real queuing. Above all, it requires perseverance, and it seemed that the people of Petrozavodsk had plenty of it. I often took Pirjo with me, if the weather permitted; she counted as a queuer and got the same ration as I did.

There were sometimes as many as ten separate queues in the hall, and a clever queuer could join up to three of them. This was achieved by standing in one queue for a couple of hours, then leaving a child or another relative to keep your place, and then running backwards and forwards like that from one queue to another.

Waiting in line for hour after hour left me completely exhausted. I had a temperamental, tired and hungry girl with me and she often had a tantrum on the way home – queuing in the winter was hardly much fun for an adult, let alone a 6-year-old. But it couldn't be helped. Who wouldn't have cursed this situation?

'Why oh why are the goods not just put on a rationing card instead of expecting us to queue up all the time? Standing like this in your thin clothing in the cold and the frost and the wind could kill you. Shivering here night after night, even the strong ones will weaken and become prone to diseases.' Thus spoke an old American Finn who had brought thousands of dollars' worth of machines, supplies and goods with him when he entered the country.

I asked the same thing to a party member, although I already knew the answer.

'Well! The card system is useful when stocks of goods are low and depleted, and when there is no clear information about when they will be replenished. But our country isn't suffering from a shortage of goods. In fact, we have much more purchasing power than we realise, which is, of course, due to the well-being of the people and the elimination of unemployment. It's just that our congested transportation system cannot transport and distribute goods to the extent necessary. In time, things will improve. In addition, military transportation now takes priority; let's not forget, we are waging a war against our rabid neighbours. Once they have been destroyed, our country will be greater and more prosperous.'

'By then, my good man, many of us will have had our limbs stiffened permanently after freezing our malnourished corpses in these eternal queues looping endlessly round the market halls, shops and kiosks,' I thought to myself.

It was the first day of March before I went back to work after being on sick leave in January, on my own pay for two weeks, and sacrificing another two weeks of summer leave. But I wanted to get the rest I needed after such a strenuous illness. At the same time, I received another invitation to donate blood, but I didn't go – I reckoned I had already given enough.

Martti wrote regularly and expressed concern about my health. As for him, he'd been spending his time in Petsamo, 'resting'. They had nothing to do but eat their meals, sit around and maybe listen to the *politruks* wittering on, which was highly amusing to all the Finnish men who'd grown up elsewhere. Those unintentional comedians' grasp of geography was pitiable. But that was common in Russia. I remember once at work being taken aback by a young Karelian girl and her comrade desperately looking at a map trying to find New York along the coasts of Portugal, France, Belgium and the Netherlands, saying, 'I thought it was supposed to be on the Atlantic coast somewhere?' She was an intelligent enough girl, as was her companion, both having attended school for several years.

The boys in Petsamo received regular food and vodka to keep both the cold and the resentment at bay.

'I once saved up half a litre of vodka, even though that's strictly forbidden,' Martti told me in his letter. 'I exchanged it for the same amount of tinned milk which one of the lads had acquired somewhere.'

They did not have any information about the course that the war was taking, save to say that the Red Army was crushing all before it and was marching towards Helsinki.

32

March 1940

On 13 March 1940, I arrived for my morning shift at the usual time. I was confronted with a huge commotion, people roaring and shouting, but I couldn't make any sense of it at first. Everyone looked flabbergasted and couldn't put two sensible words together. But eventually I heard: 'Peace was agreed with the Finnish Government last night.' But which Finnish Government might that be? The Terijoki Government or the Helsinki one? I mean, for months now, Molotov had been declaring that he recognised only the People's Government headed by Kuusinen.[36] So what about now? The Kuusinen Government had fallen, and peace had been negotiated with the previous strict bourgeois government. Well, well! What about that march in Helsinki? And what about all those staged behind-the-scenes images of the People's Army in their green uniforms? Why had peace talks even become a possibility? Molotov's natural benevolence? My head was spinning.

---

36 The People's Government refers to the Terijoki Government which was formed at the start of the Winter War. This government represented the Finnish Democratic Republic which was supposed to become a socialist state after the Soviet Union claimed victory of the Winter War. The Terijoki Government had signed agreements with Molotov in December 1939 but, as the war did not progress as planned, Moscow began negotiations with the true Finnish Government.

Our old defector friend, an American Finn, didn't seem to be making much sense of it either: 'So peace has been agreed, has it? What use is peace now? There's been a total revolution there, and Kuusinen is sorting things out in Helsinki – clearing up all the mess everyone else has made.'

I laughed out loud at this. The old man obviously needed some help joining the dots: 'Don't be ridiculous. I don't think you can call Ryti, Walden and Paasikivi revolutionaries, can you? And they're the ones that Molotov has negotiated the peace with.'

'But ... but ... Molotov only just said that no one but Kuusinen ...' stuttered the old man.

'I don't really understand either, to be honest: there's something not quite right there. But, yes, I think Molotov has changed his mind, because we're not hearing anything about the People's Government any more. If Kuusinen's Government has failed ...'

'Shut up about that! I just want to know about the terms,' he barked at me angrily.

'Well, it means an awful lot of Finland being handed over to the Soviet Union. Of the cities, certainly Vyborg, Priozersk and Sortavala for a start. Gogland and Bolshoy Tyuters as well. The whole Hanko Peninsula is to be leased out.'

'Dear God!' said the old man under his breath as he left, a baffled and disbelieving look on his face.

Anyway, I was in better spirits. Peace was a great thing, after all, and Finland, for the most part, had been saved. When I got home, I told Pirjo that peace had come and her father would be allowed to come home soon. Pirjo shook her small blonde head indifferently and waved her hand precociously: 'I knew that even before you told me.'

'Oh really? Where did you hear that from?' I replied in my amazement.

'The old lady at the crèche told us this morning that the Zinns had been defeated and now they can't come and kill us and do evil things. And then she said that all the children's daddies would come home.'

'But my sweet child, what on earth is a Zinn?'

'Don't you know? It's those Finns,' the girl explained.

'But *we* are all Finns: me, Daddy, you ...'

'Yes, but we're not the ones trying to take over.'

'Did the lady tell you that?'

'Yes she did and she said that no one should tease me for being a Finn, even if you can't speak Russian.'

'Hmm ... is that so?'

I felt hemmed in: in the moment I was struggling to come up with a way of explaining things to the girl. At the crèche, it looked like they were leading children down the approved political path.

By this point Pirjo was at a new crèche near our apartment. The facility was generally well run, all the staff consisting of older women who looked less like the political nutcases you got in a lot of the other facilities. The food was good, and there were regular medical check-ups. The childcare workers had been thoroughly nice to me, despite my poor language skills. For the summer, the whole crèche facility took its children and moved to the countryside, a unique benefit not available at the other facilities in the city. But I was still taken aback by what Pirjo had just come out with.

For a long time the peace settlement gave the newspapers, radio and political enthusiasts plenty to talk about. But soldiers' families still waited in vain for their men to return. Although the People's Army had been disbanded, men had been transferred into the ranks of the Red Army in various other locations. They were kept busy doing rifle drills and kept in the dark about when they would be discharged. I couldn't help but wonder if all of this was actually a rehearsal for the next act in the play.

It wasn't until the last day of June that Martti came home – one of the first out of his troop to do so. Sporting a green hat which bore the People's Army coat of arms and was covered with lice and dirt, he marched in out of the scorching heat. They had taken the rest of his People's Army uniform back.

'In honour of Antikainen,[37] we will leave in organised ranks and make our way to the celebration at Kirov Square,' the political

---

37 Toivo Antikainen, a Finnish-born communist and a military officer in the Soviet Red Army.

head of the artel announced one day in early summer. The Russian women in our workshop didn't particularly take to this idea. Someone casually remarked something about letting the Finns celebrate it if they wanted to. But it was loud enough for the *politruk* to hear, who flew into a rage and at the top of his voice gave an impassioned speech about the suffering of a 'great Finnish man', whose release from a life in prison came only by the intervention of great Stalin himself. It was hardly asking too much for everyone to sacrifice an hour or two of their afternoon to form a welcome party for such a man.

But someone next to us still dared to mumble, 'If it were only today, then fine: but there'll only be another meeting of some sort tomorrow or else we'll be celebrating something different. You always have to leave your home unattended — and your kids as well.'

But the *politruk* either didn't hear it or pretended not to hear it.

The Kirov market was full of people, as it always was when you were all required to go straight from work to join the throng. At the base of the statue were the members of the welcoming committee and other dignitaries. Antikainen was there, as were Taimi,[38] Kuusinen, Kupriyanov,[39] Lehén[40] and many others. Everyone was talking about Antikainen and Taimi, of course. A band struck up from time to time. Antikainen himself gave a speech in Russian reading directly from his notes. A special reception for Antikainen was later held for Finns in the courtyard of the former cooperative houses along Uritski Street. Antikainen spoke for over an hour. He is easier to listen to than a lot of the other preachers of communism, whose speeches contain not the slightest mark of originality. They're all afraid to say anything of their own in case it comes back to bite them when the powers-that-be get to hear it.

---

38 Adolf Taimi, a Finnish–Soviet Bolshevik and one of the founding members of the Communist Party of Finland.
39 Gennady Kupriyanov, a Soviet politician who served as the First Secretary of the Communist Party of the Karelo–Finnish–Soviet Socialist Republic from 1940 to 1950.
40 Tuure Lehén, a Finnish–Soviet politician and also journalist and historian.

March 1940

Antikainen talked a lot about Finnish prison conditions, inadvertently criticising the Soviet prison authorities. He talked up the freedoms that Finnish prisoners enjoyed: freedoms that would never be granted here. For example, he had been allowed to meet his sister in the prison manager's office. How many people gathered here who were relatives of detainees would have envied that lucky sister who got to visit her brother in prison? The people here of course had no idea what had happened to their relatives, not having seen them since the night they were imprisoned, years ago in many cases. Never mind being allowed to send magazines, books and packages to the prison – things that Antikainen was grateful to have received. You couldn't help but see the difference! Antikainen also described how the escorting Finnish officer had bid him farewell at the last border post, 'Goodbye, Antikainen!'

Antikainen had turned to him and replied, 'Don't count your chickens, sir. When we come back, it won't be kids' stuff, believe you me!'

Tuure Lehén translated Antikainen's speech into Russian. After the meeting, photographers circled around Antikainen, taking shots which included ones of him surrounded by children.

We had returned to a time when you could dare to be Finnish again. 'Finnishness' had come out of hiding. It was hilarious to see newspapers and orators praising our virtues. Kupriyanov, the Karelia Party secretary, gave an outstanding speech about the beauty of the Finnish language: its classical literature and its achievements in the service of science; it was a civilised language respected by all. And – just like that – it was all forgotten: how for the last few years it had been trampled underfoot, prohibited in schools and on the stage, how they even tried to suppress it as a colloquial spoken language, demanding we all speak Russian – even if we knew nothing but Finnish.

On 6 April 1940, a new Finnish newspaper called *Totuus* (*Truth*) made its first appearance in Petrozavodsk, a version of Moscow's *Pravda*. But they had to build some sort of foundation for their new federal republic, and this was established at a session of the Supreme Soviet in Moscow, apparently to thunderous applause. The Finns and the Karelians got themselves a new government, marking the beginning of the short history of the Karelo–Finnish–Soviet Socialist Republic. Its borders encompassed the territory of the former Autonomous Republic of Karelia and the new 'Occupied Territories'. To populate this new state, people were recruited, commanded, or simply permitted to migrate there. By choice, Finns moved there all the way from Siberia, as if pulled by a strong magnet. In any case, it was a more congenial and pleasant place to live than anything Russia had to offer.

The big migration was quickly hindered by a decree of June that year, which forbade plant managers from dismissing employees solely on the basis of being late. A resignation could only be granted at the behest of the Medical Commission if an employee fell ill, if a worker was commandeered by another organisation, or if they left to study. Tardiness now met with a different punishment. Pursuant to a decision of the People's Court, a person who was late for work was fined 25 per cent of their salary for a period of between two and six months, or, in extreme cases, would go to prison for possibly a couple of months. Everyone was now essentially forced labour.

At the same time, quality requirements at work were tightened. All manufactures were subjected to rigorous inspection, with a dedicated officer in every workplace to oversee quality. If any products that he had passed ended up being returned for any reason, that would spell the end for him – and the prison doors would swing open not just for him but for the factory manager as well; and the careless employee would face percentage fine after percentage fine. It was truly punitive legislation, enough to make your hair stand on end, and people would curse under their breath. But the people had grown accustomed to everything they'd had thrown at them and they just took it in their stride, like they had done with everything else before. Powerless, all you could do was be content to play your part.

33

Summer to Autumn 1940

Because of the new labour law, Martti wasn't keen to return to his old job at the Perevalka railyard. When you were released from the military, you had the right to apply for a job anywhere. Admittedly, he would have been taken on again at his old place with all his former benefits intact, which were not insignificant. On the other hand, the work was so arduous, loading timber into railway wagons, that in the end he decided to look for lighter work elsewhere rather than submit to what, under the new law, was starting to look like a life sentence.

Around that time, we received a letter from Martti's friend who lived near Sortavala, which extolled the beauty of the place, its apartments and its job opportunities, and urged Martti to stop by at least to have a look before thinking about anything else. So off Martti went, and his letters home spoke of nothing else other than why we should relocate there. He had already found a job on a nearby island and was going to join the Finnish fishermen's brigade, despite having had no experience of fishing whatsoever. The apartment was great, he said, and the surrounding countryside better than you could possibly imagine. He urged me to quit my job straight away and get ready to move.

I wrote an application to the administration of my workplace asking permission to resign on the grounds that my husband was moving to a new area to work. The request was flatly refused. So I got a certificate proving that Martti was already contracted elsewhere, but received the same response: 'Cannot be released.' And yet I was just an ordinary worker and by no means indispensable. So I threatened the leader with civil court if he continued to disrupt my family life with his refusal. The director convened a meeting of the administration and only then was the matter resolved in my favour. To be fair, the poor leader was just being extremely careful; he was a good-natured man who feared for his life when it came to bearing any kind of responsibility for complying with government regulations.

By 6 September, we had made it some of the way, joining another family in taking possession of a railway wagon at Petrozavodsk Station where we could stow all our belongings. This was no mean achievement, even if it meant living in a cold carriage from Sunday morning until noon the following Wednesday, before the train set off to take us to Sortavala.

Late at night, bathed in moonlight, we crossed the old border. I watched as others slept and felt strangely moved. I looked through the doorway at the roads painted silver by the moon. Crossing the border was a deeply held desire that I hadn't dared articulate clearly, even to myself.

In the morning, the train pulled in at the forlorn-looking station. It would colour your cheeks red with shame just to look at it. The disconsolate sight of protruding furnaces and scorched trees in the yards was all that was left of once such a beautiful area. And all this had been done by the country whose head of state had so piously proclaimed to the world: 'We do not desire a square foot of a foreign land, but we will not surrender an inch of our own.'

The journey was relentlessly slow. The train seemed to fall asleep at every station and struggle back into life like a knackered old horse. It took almost a week to get to Sortavala Station, from where we were fortunate to be given a car ride to our destination. I didn't get much of a chance to see the city, the car hurtled through it so quickly. The road meandered around the coast, with high cliffs rising above it. It all looked stunningly beautiful in the autumn sun.

In Nukuttalahti, our destination, the properties were huddled around a bay that cut into the island. The houses looked colourful and fun. They were adorable to set eyes on: all I'd seen for years was grey and filth. Martti's apartment was in a new-looking red house on a hill, with pines and large birch trees in the yard. The barn, the stable and the other outbuildings all had red-tiled roofs. The cottage had a large living area, its white-painted cardboard walls shining, a large oven in the corner and plenty of windows; behind were two more, smaller rooms. All the fixtures and fittings were neat and well made. There weren't any movable items left, though. But this was understandable: the house had been empty for five months, and, being right by the road, it had been cleared out by some of its thousands of passers-by.

As I explored my new surroundings with Martti that day, I had to tell him how sad it actually made me feel, settling here, where, everywhere you looked, you could see signs of the former owners. Martti admitted to having had similar thoughts, especially when he first arrived.

'Yes, absolutely that. It feels wrong. On the other hand, for our part, we can clean all of this up and repair what the looters have broken. We'll be like tenants. If we don't make this place into a home, then someone will just come along and trash everything,' he said quietly.

I was consoled by that thought as well. Encouraged, I began work on improving the house and its grounds so that, if we ever were to encounter the owners, we would have nothing to be ashamed of. There was plenty to do. First of all, the well needed cleaning out; there was a terrible stench coming out of it. Martti, with the help of our friend who lived in the other small room at the back, emptied it twice over, drawing out every kind of thing imaginable, even some slaughter waste that must have been down there for months. An evil, disgusting stink leached out everywhere as the well was being emptied. After being scrubbed with a stiff brush and rinsed with plenty of water, the well was finally usable. It was fairly easy to clean, in fact, as it had a rock bottom and concrete tubes for walls.

The main wall in the sauna had been demolished and the stove was gone. The benches had to be put back together again and all the rubbish removed. All the windows had to be repaired. The basement was full of rotten potatoes. There was evidence of random vandalism by passers-by everywhere you looked. And no wonder. After all, even government agents and commissioners, coming all the way from Moscow, acting on orders or not, had been sniffing around here, helping themselves to anything not nailed down. Even the door furniture had been removed, and fitted cabinets and window frames had been stripped out. Young hooligans had bragged about their rampages: the number of houses where they'd smashed the windows in. The officials did make some effort to prohibit such malicious damage, but what good would that do in the midst of all this chaos?

Shortly after the peace talks, the commissions had commandeered the property of shops and private individuals – and how much of that was never seen again? A director from Petrozavodsk had been on a train earlier that summer, returning from a mission to Leningrad and Vyborg, and had overheard a conversation between two commanders' wives who were sitting next to some very full suitcases. The two women were delighted about how many trips from Leningrad they'd been able to make to see their men in Vyborg.

'Eighteen times I've done this journey to see Kolya,' one of them chirped.

'If she'd been dragging all that plunder back with her every time, it's not hard to see where everything in Vyborg is ending up,' said the director resentfully.

Some goods ended up in Petrozavodsk as well, of course, sold for commission: imported sewing machines, coats, shoes ... everything. People desperate for things just pounced on them. They were bagging their places in the queues the night before, and, when the stores opened in the morning, in they went, barging through the doors. One day, a petite woman got pushed over and trampled so badly that, when the medic arrived on the scene, nothing could be done for her. After that incident, the militia took control and put up wire fences to force the buyers into line. They even introduced the ridiculous system of writing a queue number on the back of everyone's hand with a copying pen.[41] All the same, it was considered a brilliant idea

---

41 The ink in these pens was highly toxic.

as it helped maintain order. Of course, the best goods went to the big cities, and some transactions probably happened in secret through the side doors. Still, the people of Petrozavodsk were happy just to be able to buy something after having queued for so long.

Life in Nukuttalahti soon found a regular rhythm. Martti went out to the outer islands every Monday with the fishermen, and I was left in peace with my girl all week. The house was soon all in order and I had more free time than I had could have dreamt of in all those long years. I went for walks with Pirjo and I got to know my new neighbours. Most of them had come here from either America or Canada; there were a couple of Ingrian Finnish families, and there were some like us who had originally come from Finland. There was not a single fisherman among the menfolk; only later did an American chap with fishing experience join the brigade, which was led by a cheerful Karelian with little if any knowledge of fishing. Of course, they didn't come back with any fish. That was partly due to their lousy equipment, but the biggest obstacle was unfamiliar waters. The men were reallocated from one place to another but with meagre results. It was spring before some fish were finally caught.

So the salaries couldn't be paid, as stipulated by the contracts, and the dissatisfaction was palpable. Everyone tried to cope the best they could. Most people in Sortavala had a cow, and you got a good price for the milk, which helped families survive. Some of the women took in sewing from the people on a nearby collective farm or from the city. Those who had savings had to live on them, for the men's salary on its own – 166 roubles a month – wouldn't keep a family. And it wasn't possible to get out of your work contract once you'd signed up to it.

Our small village was just populated by fishermen. I don't think any of the houses suffered from neglect: everyone repaired and did up their house using whatever skills they had and whatever materials they could lay their hands on. In the surrounding villages, it wasn't such a pretty picture. In true Russian style, broken windows had been covered with rags, or else blocked up completely. Timber from out-buildings, even from houses, was being used for firewood. It was that infuriating Russian laziness again: not bothering to step out of your surroundings and look for firewood a bit further away while you can get it nearer and with less effort. It's the same laziness and lethargy that means you have to have a waterless toilet with its contents in the same building where you live and eat. Whole houses were stripped and left to rot. Even the trees in the yard, right outside the front door, were cut down.

Sortavala was still a beautiful place, although the burnt-out buildings were a reminder of how much more pristine and beautiful it had once been. But there was plenty still to be proud of. Nothing was allowed to look scruffy for want of a coat of paint, and there were no ugly sides of buildings to be seen. Pirjo was even more enchanted by it than I was. Even at 7 years old she was already showing signs of a very independent and inquisitive mind.

When we had just arrived, she asked me, 'Mummy, I don't understand: why did they go and leave their homes?'

'Well, because, well, I don't know – I suppose they had to.'

'Who made them?'

'Oh, darling, the war, the war. And don't ask me right now, I can't explain it you.'

It really would have been quite a lovely story, wouldn't it, if I explained to her all about the turmoil, the pain and the powerlessness, the futile hopes burning inside me, and if she, in her naivety, tried to enlighten her little friends. This could have quite easily led to an invitation to the refuge of the NKVD and the possibility of disappearing there forever; people had gone there and not come back for expressing much less illicit thoughts than those. You always had to think about what you were saying; you had to be careful wherever you went.

It seemed like a lot of Finns from other parts of the Soviet Union had moved to Sortavala as well. How many more might have arrived if the state of the housing had been more favourable and the city council had issued residence permits? The beauty and cleanliness of the city was an attractive proposition. However, a lot of people were whispering cautiously about how long that cleanliness would last; before long, wouldn't everything just end up looking Russian – *all the same*?

Summer to Autumn 1940

And, yes, I had time on my hands and things to read. Books and magazines were to be found all over the place here. For many years now, I had barely read anything for enjoyment – particularly after the Great Purge had taken its toll, I had been desperately pining for something to read. The relentless destruction of books back then was so distressing. Anyone with even the least anxiety burnt the entire contents of their bookshelves. The Uritski Street Barracks' toilet facilities were inundated with them. Torn and strewn across the floor lay hundreds of valuable and beautifully bound Finnish- and English-language textbooks imported from America, along with historical and literary works, with not a soul to speak up for them. Quite the opposite: everyone was hastily bringing their own collection to add to the pile, the wisest course of action. One *politruk* thought it best to destroy every single Finnish-language book, whether printed locally or imported. 'There's just no way of knowing what's acceptable any more,' he said.

I was one of the few who overcame my fear. I never destroyed my books, not even then. I mean, there weren't very many, probably a few dozen, mostly to remind me of Kari and Aarno. Besides, I used to consider myself such a hot property, and inevitably heading for prison, that I let my books remain on my shelf as a gesture of defiance. Later, during the war, I even acquired more through an acquaintance of mine.

Now I was in Nukuttalahti I had plenty of books. Martti had picked them up whenever he saw them lying around with no one claiming ownership. Some were bound and some had no cover, some torn, some intact, some rain damaged, some pristine – all forbidden literature and condemned to the bonfire. I devoured them with such ardour, even though many lacked their opening and closing pages. I don't think I've ever read that much in such a short time.

One day I was looking at an issue of *Suomen Kuvalehti* that I'd not seen before; in fact, it had been ages since I'd seen a copy of that magazine at all. It just happened to open up at the centre pages, revealing several pictures of the Helsinki bombings. It was a shock. I felt unable to comprehend what the text and the pictures were telling me. It turned out that Helsinki had in fact been deliberately targeted by bombing. I quickly scanned the rest of the issue, glanced through several others, and, still feeling stunned, went to search for Martti. I showed him the pictures and read the accompanying story. There it was: Finnish cities behind the battle lines – Helsinki, little Porvoo, Mikkeli and several others – had all been bombed anyway.

'How awful is that? And to think we once believed what Molotov was telling America. How can he stand up and tell such barefaced lies to the whole world? Betray his own people?' So the conversation with Martti went. It was unforgivably wrong – a cruel and deliberate crime which I wasn't prepared to forget about. Despite my tendency to be cautious, I couldn't help myself from showing the magazines to a few of my closest neighbours; they were horrified, too. I mean, the magazines could be found anywhere – they were hard to avoid. But when you picked them up and took them somewhere else, well, then they were dangerous. Someone once took some copies to Petrozavodsk. Another person picked one up and, without thinking, took it to his workplace. The political 'eye' reported the matter to the relevant institutions, and that was all it took for the man to be incarcerated for many years and deported. One time, a young locally born Petrozavodsk newspaper man came by an issue of *Suomen Kuvalehti*; it was given to him purely as an example of magnificent typesetting and technical excellence. The journalist took care to lock the issue away in his safe, but someone must have caught sight of it and reported him. Sooner or later, the NKVD men picked him up and put him away. He was sentenced to five years, and neither his influential siblings nor his father were able to get the sentence commuted.

34

Spring to Summer 1941

Some 1.5km from Nukuttalahti there was a farm collective, which as far as I can recall was called 'Komintern'. Its members had been moved here from central Russia under semi-compulsory recruitment and weren't used to their new environment. Of course, their apartments were better than they'd had back home. But why did the Finns have to build their houses so far apart? They just couldn't understand it. In Russian villages, houses sit side by side on both sides of the road and you don't see any grass until the houses stop and the fields begin. Well, they had a lot to ponder about and reasons to feel homesick.

'We can't live here,' an old, bearded chap said, sorrowfully. 'These Finns have all been craftsmen, shoemakers, carpenters – and who knows what other kind of jobs they did on the side. There are professional tools in all their houses. We're just farmers: we've got nothing in common with these artisans. And what about all these fields? What kinds of fields do you call these, mountains on one side and rocks on the other? You should see our fields at home!'

They continued to grumble along these lines and did what they could to get back to what they were used to. It seems that their agreements must have allowed them to return to their former farm collectives if they wanted, seeing as so many of them ended up leaving Karelia. All the state demanded was a one-off payment: a few hundred roubles to be handed over when they signed the release. But the cost of the journey home had to come out of their own pockets and it wasn't cheap. To get the money for the fee and the return journey, they sold their livestock off at sale prices. That spring, Sortavala Market looked like a Sunday farmers' market, with pigs, cows and smaller animals all joining the noisy chorus.

New recruits for the farm collective were brought in from all over Russia. By May, huge swathes of newcomers occupied both sides of the railway track. For several days, they camped out under open skies, shivering in the cold spring frost, until the slow-turning administrative wheels eventually meant it was their turn and put them where they belonged.

Life in Sortavala gradually came together. Shops opened here and there, and getting hold of goods was much easier here than in Petrozavodsk. We islanders ran from store to store to join the queues.

In the spring, all Finnish men under the age of 25 who had not received any military training in the national army were called up to enter the reserves. Accordingly, a couple of men left our fishing team and were fetched up first at a training camp in Perkjärvi. Manoeuvres were only supposed to last a couple of months, but this was extended and the men were billeted in faraway Estonia; no more information was forthcoming about when they were coming home. Then the war came and many men were still conscripted; we would just have to wait and see if they were ever going to return to their families again, even as prisoners of war.

As May Day approached, I took a trip to Petrozavodsk to try to drum up some cash. The fishing didn't really put enough food on the table, all our savings had been spent and life was looking increasingly bleak. So, to try to improve the situation, I thought I would try to sell Martti's second-best suit. It wasn't a wasted journey. Life in Petrozavodsk seemed to be carrying on very much as before. It was a little easier to get food now, but you could still see queues. I didn't stay in town for long. When I'd done what I came to do, I made my way back, finding a travel companion in my old acquaintance, Commander Toivo Viima. He was one of those brave friends of mine from the old days; I'd got to know him while Kari was still alive. And he hadn't had an easy time of it either, although the sun seemed to be shining on him again these days. He'd married my friend Aune, now a young chemistry and physics teacher, a couple of months after they'd met at my place following Aarno's arrest. Toivo had received a transfer to a small West Siberian garrison town, and, after graduating from university, Aune travelled to see him. Two years later, in 1938, the same day their little daughter celebrated her first birthday, Toivo was imprisoned. Aune returned to Petrozavodsk with her child and got a teaching position in the countryside nearby. The following summer, Toivo turned up at his mother-in-law's, looking ragged and emaciated. By some miracle, he had been released from prison. He related how he had already been given his death sentence along with some other commanders but, for whatever reason, it was never carried out. At this point things started to take a turn for the better. His case was taken up again because his former interrogator had ended up behind bars himself, where he had admitted that 'the Finn had been quite impossible, refusing to sign his name on the interrogation records neither willingly nor under coercion'. So the interrogator had ended up signing them himself. Toivo's unit, the political commissar of the troops and the commander were all asked to give new statements, and the difference between these and the old ones was remarkable. Now Toivo had all the virtues and repute of a great commander conferred upon him, whereas in the previous round of statements these same men had purportedly fallen over themselves to discredit this corrupt, wretched excuse for an officer.

'So one morning there it was: a travel ticket and permission to go home to my wife.'

'Did they beat you in there?' I asked.

'I was forced to stand an awful lot, for hours on end. I'll never forget that as long as I live. There were ninety intellectuals in this one small room, including judges, commanders and others from the same district. One judge said he had been ordered to scour the district and flush out predetermined percentages of vermin, subversives and counter-revolutionaries. He had been appalled. Arguing that he couldn't meet quotas like this without augmenting the numbers with the innocent, he promptly refused. That gesture earned him a place alongside the rest of the accused. The room was crammed full of people, and being interrogated while being forced to constantly stand was destroying the man's spirit.'

Toivo went back to his wife in the countryside and became a full-time carer for his child. For a couple of months he was left in peace. Then they began calling up Finns and Karelians into the People's Army, Toivo included. Life was starting to look up. As a Red officer in the People's Army, he was decorated like a Christmas tree. After the war, he was promoted to a senior lieutenant's position in the regular army in Medvezhyegorsk. And, just like that, an inmate on death row becomes a commander again.

When spring came, I threw myself into my gardening. Having perused my old books for instructions, I set to tilling the ground with a hoe for days at a time, forking manure from a wheelbarrow and tending my fruit bushes. I managed to create cute-looking rows of different vegetables. I fought for their survival in their battle against the chickens and replanted my peas three times until they flourished. My enthusiasm was unshakeable.

'I don't know why you're bothering,' said my next-door neighbour, a jolly, rotund woman. 'Who knows how long we'll be staying here on this money? You're wearing yourself out for nothing.'

'Ah yes, but what if everyone had that attitude? What would happen to the poor land?' I refuted.

'Fair enough. But the men's wages are so hopeless that it stops you wanting to try.'

It was in fact futile as it turned out, because, just at the point when my flowerbeds and vegetable patches needed watering and weeding, I had to leave them to their own devices. Summer was at its most beautiful. It was as glorious here as anywhere. It all spoke of peace and continuity. But how deceiving that was.

The thought often crossed our minds about what would happen if war were waged on these lands again. We would be evacuated, of course. But what if you decided to take your chances and stay and hide? Could the Finns ever accept the fact that we had been living in their houses? I mean, we weren't the ones who had forced them out. On the contrary, we felt only the deepest sympathy for anyone displaced from their home. And, being Finns, we'd all done our best, at least in this village, to keep everything in good order. But all musings about a potential war were banished when the actual war began.

Molotov's speech was broadcast everywhere, and it was our group leader who told us about it late one Sunday night, while announcing that he, too, would be required to join up. In the days that followed, the streets of Sortavala were full of weeping women, children and elderly alongside their menfolk who were off to join the war. The commanders straight away packed their families off with all their belongings out of the city. But it was 30 June before all the various work facilities told the mothers with children to pack only the essentials and be ready to go to designated points along the railway track. Most of the men and childless women had already been assigned fortification work near the border.

Day after day you would see an inconsolable group of mothers, children and old folk standing by the track next to their belongings waiting for the wagons. The *politruks* tried to reassure us, saying nobody knew if we were really in any danger, but it was a good idea to go somewhere else for a couple of months. Later, the crowds were transported in great barges along Lake Ladoga and River Syväri to the other side of Lake Onega somewhere towards the Vologda area.

Several times we received notifications as well: get all the women and children ready with immediate effect. Nobody wanted to leave. Waiting for the final order was making me anxious. All of our little community seemed to be boiling and frothing. The men's wages still hadn't come in and everything seemed messed up. Cattle and goods from the farm collectives were being transported up and down night and day.

The men finally reached an agreement with the city council that our group would leave in its entirety on fishing vessels and take the fishing brigade's most valuable property with them to the Olonets region. That was one crumb of comfort: at least families would be staying together. On the morning of 6 July, the cattle crew left on foot. There were thirteen cows altogether, all privately owned, as well as some sheep; only the two horses were communal property. The women led their cows and cast longing gazes behind them. The 180km journey that lay ahead was going to be strenuous for many, certainly for the older women, but they made a brisk start. Along the way, some of the cows fell ill, all manner of other kinds of misfortunes befell them, and at times these overwrought and emotional women were almost pulling each other's hair out in their heated arguments. But in the end they all made it.

For the rest of us the journey started just a couple of days later. It happened to be my birthday, and I don't think I've ever spent a birthday feeling so mournful and crying so much. It was so hard to have to part from all the beautiful things that I had seen here and among which I had been allowed to live, and to head towards my sombre future.

One by one, another boat crew was ready to go, so I did one more tour of my house and the grounds. Everything was in good order. I had planted my flowers out in an empty flower bed: the roses I'd brought back from Petrozavodsk, my fuchsias, and all the others that I'd not had the heart to drag inside to dry. At least if they were outside under the open sky, the rain and sun would take care of them.

I was convinced that, as soon as we left the beach, the remaining townspeople and the rural Russians would be stampeding all over the place, taking everything they could carry, destroying, smashing, shattering and defiling. It was so difficult to leave.

35

Summer 1941

One by one, the boats embarked from the shore with their full cargoes and the journey began. The smaller animals and pigs had their own boxes. It was amusing to begin with to listen to them grunting and moving around, but as the journey went on the boxes began to stink unbearably in the hot weather. It would have been absolutely intolerable if we hadn't kept cleaning them out, as difficult as that was without any peat. I observed the crew on my boat. It consisted solely of one Finnish man, Kalle, who had come to the Soviet Union from America, my Pirjo, who managed to sleep through all the bad weather with the boat rocking and swaying, myself and otherwise just a dozen chickens and a goat. The goods were piled high in the middle.

'We might end up sinking, Kaarina,' said Kalle, comfortingly, seated at the stern. 'I'm no seaman: I've not really seen much water before I got to Nukuttalahti. Let's see if I can work out how to steer using this spade thing.'

With trepidation I looked at this 'spade' of his: a paddle which required all the strength in your wrists just to move it. The other paddle was at hand in case this one snapped into pieces. He was a forester by trade, but he was up to the job despite the ferocious, high waves, and he even goofed around a little from time to time. Martti was the coxswain in a large motorless boat on which the men had fashioned a mast and sails and some remarkably large oars. There were seven boats in all, with twenty-nine people in them; ten had been left to drive the cattle.

Lake Ladoga showed us all the facets of its personality. It could be serenely beautiful, dead calm, forcing us to use the oars in the scorching heat. It also stormed and thundered as strong as it could muster, causing the stern of the boat to disappear into the foam and our little wooden box to groan and creak as if it were going to fall apart. The sweat poured down from Kalle's temples, the goat grunted and looked for safety by poking its head under the hem of my skirt, but my darling Pirjo slept as if she were in her own bed. It was awful to watch those foam-headed waves attacking each other in the angry lake: every time the boat dipped down to the bottom of a wave, your eyes closed instinctively. But then we just ploughed further forward, our ragged, rotten sails howling.

When we looked back, we often wondered how we avoided suffering any damage along the way. Almost all the women had been seasick. A couple of times we almost ran aground. Once, in the worst storm at the mouth of the Tuulosjoki River, a couple of the boats that were carrying pigs almost got lost with the men on board, but fortunately they were helped into a more sheltered area.

At the mouth of the Olonka River, the cattle crew were waiting for us with their herd. We spent a few days in pine huts. The men reported to the military authorities and looked for a place where we could stay. There was a village nearby with a burnt-out sawmill, and that's where we were assigned. But the men put up a vehement resistance: Lake Ladoga was miles away from there, there was a strong upstream current to row against in the river, and the area was covered with drifted sand, allowing not the slightest opportunity for cattle grazing. So we were given permission to move to the ancient monastery of Ontrova.[42]

The monastery, which for years had been a residence for border guards, was poetically beautiful. The ruins of the old church, the perimeter walls and the corner chapels were verdant and resplendent.

---

42 Known today as the St Adrian of Ondrusov Monastery.

Summer 1941

Old maples and linden trees whispered as if it were still the ancient days of the pious monks. You couldn't help but feel the ghosts of the past as you walked around.

We were allowed to stay there to get ourselves through the winter. The men unloaded the boats and carried the cargo up to the homes, which had been allocated to the different families, but not before some arguments had broken out. The women cleaned and arranged their belongings. Over the next few days, all the goods that had been drenched in the storm were dried out, and the laundry was done. Life was starting to look organised. That lasted for four days.

In the morning a strict order came to move on before nightfall. The village of Ilyinski was being vacated already. The now familiar routine began of dragging our possessions to the shore and hauling them onto boats. Everyone slaughtered all their pigs and chickens – after all, we had no idea where we were going to end up. We took up our travels again late that evening and by the next morning we had reached the mouth of the Pisi River. The whole river mouth was a huge cluster of vessels: dozens of evacuee boats with their heavy loads, like it was fish market day. Everywhere was crowded: the banks of the river, the surrounding woods, under upturned boats on the shore, and inside the barns. People kept on coming by boat and even more on foot, driving cattle and carrying their possessions. We had to stay here; we hadn't got permission to go any further. The only place you were allowed to bed down was in a nearby village, if you were lucky enough to find anywhere. We remained on the shore. Everyone either stayed in the huts where the nets were smoke-cleaned or in the sheds used to store fishing gear.

The journey from Sortavala to Pisi had taken twenty days in all, including stops. Here, no one was going to bother taking their things out of the boats, at least not in the first few days. Instead, guards were deployed in shifts to stop passers-by grabbing anything. You just lived one day at a time.

Not much was known about the war. The most insane rumours were circulating. But reckless talk was best avoided; you just had to wait and see. While we were there, a handsome old Karelian man, who looked rather like Väinämöinen from the *Kalevala* folk tale, was arrested precisely because of one careless utterance. I found out later that he had said to some telltale or other: 'I expect we'll be able to cope living with the Finns, seeing as we've managed to live with the Russians all this time.'

One morning I woke up to a loud conversation. A fisherman from Pisi village was informing everyone that all men born after 1897 were obliged to register with the Pisi Village Council: they were changing the conscription age. That's what I had been expecting all along. Families would end up being broken apart in the midst of this war, no matter what. The men left, just the six of them. Their broken-hearted families stayed behind. 'There's nothing you can do,' I said to myself, quietly contemplating the future.

There was little food, certainly no sources from which you could gather any significant stocks. Any bread you could buy from the village came following permission from the village council, granted only after loud complaining. Rations got continuously smaller until finally the children were on 200g a day. The cow owners at least had milk, and my kind goat helped keep my Pirjo alive.

After a few days, our men returned, all but the young Finn from Ingria. Their papers were stamped 'Temporary', but that was enough for us. Just so our life together could continue for a little while. The men fished but caught little. Eating seemed to have become quite a luxury. A distant explosion informed us that the battle was within range. It was rumoured that the Finns had reached the banks of the Tuulosjoki River. Sometimes at night the sky was ablaze and the rumble brought us outdoors to listen and stare.

Once again a new command came through: this time to go and work on the Olonets plains to harvest grain. All the lone women – those with no children under the age of 8 or a cow to take care of – had to go along with the men to the Olonets farm collective's fields. At least they'll get some food there, said those who were left behind to console themselves.

To begin with, there hadn't been any kind of settlement at the mouth of the Pisi River: just fishermen from Pisi village's farm collective spending the occasional night there in a couple of small barracks. There were a few drying huts, as well as a couple of storage shelters and fish sheds. Karelian evacuees colonised the barracks, while other families went into the village. Our troops took over one hut and a storage shelter, one end of which was open and covered only by a large sail. The cows were tied up under trees for the night.

Some of those who had gone to Olonets came back to persuade their families to come and 'work for bread' as well. But Martti strictly forbade me to leave. As far as he reckoned, the mouth of the Pisinjoki River was so remote that he didn't expect any major warfare to find its way there. Those who had nipped back from Olonets informed us that our men — who had only been released from the army on a 'temporary' basis — had again been called up to rejoin. Yet a couple of days later the men themselves were informed in letters delivered by hand that they were still not expected for duty. Maybe the Finns weren't considered reliable soldiers as the battle front drew nearer?

The village authorities came over to announce that, by law, no one was allowed to go anywhere by themselves, not even families following their men to Olonets. You had to have a permit from the village council to travel on the roads. Soon, a new *ukase*[43] was issued, according to which everyone had to go to work in the village fields. A bit later, the district secretary himself even came to inspect and make a note of those we still had left. The very next day he turned up again in a menacing mood and demanded that we gather round, whereupon he ordered the cow owners to march to Mikhaylovsk and the rest of us to go by car to Lodeynoye Pole and Syväri. The Karelians raised a lot of good points in response, and made a lot of fuss, but, after the man had gone, they picked themselves up and trotted off to the village.

Our distraught women pleaded that the journey must be delayed until they could get word to their families — their daughters and their husbands — to tell them to come and pick up at least some of their clothes. The answer was a resounding 'No!' So they asked if they could be allowed to take the clothes themselves, but the response was

---

43 A decree with the force of law.

the same. The guards on the road would apparently arrest anyone who didn't have the right permit. Some set out on their own anyway to try their luck along the forest roads.

I wrote to Martti, giving my letter to those ladies who were attempting to deliver the messages. I explained how I really needed to consider leaving here, but when you're only allowed 100kg per adult and 60kg per child, how was I supposed to manage?

Having walked all through the night, the women made it to the fields and managed to talk it through with the chairman of the local farm collective. When he came to appreciate the situation, he immediately released many of the girls from work, and even allowed a few of the men to help us get ready for our journey, Martti being one of them. In the meantime, a couple of cars had arrived to pick us up. But some of the women weren't to be found and it wasn't clear how the cattle were going to be transported either. We refused to leave. A couple of hours later, another car turned up and out stepped the secretary of the village council, a young Karelian girl. She was very agitated and threatened us with all sorts of things if we didn't set off right now. I had previously heard her speaking fluently in a Karelian dialect, but now she affected not to understand a word of it.

'Speak Russian,' she insisted, haughtily.

'You should be ashamed of lying like that and denying your own mother tongue,' I snapped back at her, jittery with nerves, although I had the other women backing me up. And still we refused to leave.

Angrily, the young lady got back in her car and left, still threatening us with anything she could think of.

For days on end there was no bread, not even for the children. This couldn't go on; everyone's nerves were on edge. At night, the roar of the cannons stopped a lot of us from sleeping, and you could see the artillery fire over Lake Ladoga. It often crossed my mind that Martti had got it wrong in calling this area remote. Although it was far from any main roads and from settlements in general, the battle front could just as easily move along the riverbanks. I was disturbed from such thoughts by the arrival of Martti himself, along with some others.

Summer 1941

Martti didn't look even remotely anxious: he radiated the same calm as he always did.

He spoke to me in his usual slow, quiet manner: 'First of all, you don't need to worry. At least for now, we're not going anywhere. The fishing brigade has apparently been merged with another similar company. It's rumoured that all these fishermen will be transferred somewhere near Vologda. Although I suppose it's all a bit too late. Well ... as long as the elder of the brigade makes it back from Petrozavodsk where he's been sorting out everyone's pay among other things ... we'll see.'

That evening, while everyone else was asleep, Martti and I continued whispering to each other for ages.

'Kaarina, I think the wisest course of action now is just to be calm and wait. If an order comes to flee, then we can quietly drop back and disappear from the group. I know of a lake – more like a pond – a couple of miles from here. We're best off staying by the bank there to wait for what comes.'

'You know,' I said quietly, 'I don't believe any of those newspaper reports that talk about threats of persecution or violence by the Finns. But sometimes I can't help thinking about them.'

Martti paused thoughtfully before answering, 'If the Finns have already made it this far, then you would have to imagine they have the kind of discipline that makes for a victorious army. And discipline prohibits acts of vandalism. Discipline only disintegrates in a fleeing army, not in a victorious one.'

36

Late Summer 1941

There were only sixteen of us left. The others had already moved to somewhere near Olonets either by choice or under orders. We were still living in our little shed, illuminated by what little light snuck through the vent. We had brought our belongings in by now, which made it feel very cramped. We couldn't heat the shed because the stove would fill it with smoke, so we found ourselves frequently taken aback by how cold it was, especially at night. To varying degrees, we all looked like hillbillies now; it gave us a laugh to see each other like this, but we soon got used to it. As the end of the second month drew nigh, there was no change in sight. This wasn't what you would call living: we were just getting by the best we could, one day at a time, eating whatever we could find.

The youngest among us was only 1 year old: a little girl called Rauni, who went from one knee to the next, as carefree and happy as you like. None of it affected her: not her father's absence, serving in the Red Army somewhere far away, nor her mother's depression and regular bouts of weeping. Rauni just went on babbling.

Pirjo played all the time with her little friend Eva, who was about the same age and whose mother was also mourning the loss of her husband to the Red Army. But you could see the reality of the current situation reflected in the girls' games. As they played with their dolls, wearing their ever-present backpacks, they were evacuees or grieving mothers or little female carers.

Otherwise, it was mostly adults. An old couple lived (if you could call it living) with their 17-year-old daughter Erna in the corner of the doorway alongside their belongings; widows and their children were in the back; and our family was next to the large stove. Some of our people had gone to Olonets. There were still a couple of families in the fishing net hut and several Karelian evacuees in the barracks, along with a Finnish fisherman with his wife and 14-year-old daughter Airi.

One morning, I saw a dark cloud of smoke rising up to the skyline and expanding rapidly. I brought it to the attention of the other women when we were cooking our morning food by the campfire.

Someone said what everyone was thinking: 'I hope that's not what I think it is. Is that finally the end of the Ilyinski sawmill?'

'Last night was really awful, wasn't it,' said another. 'It felt like the whole ground was shaking from the artillery. We must be getting close to some sort of final outcome.'

Hour after hour the plume of smoke rose and spread, occupying a big part of the sky for the rest of the day, and still flaring bright red late at night. In the shadowy twilight several soldiers pushed their way across the river, some wearing Red Army uniform, others paramilitary, silent and miserable all of them. One of them confirmed that the Ilyinski sawmill was indeed on fire.

The next morning, there was a sense that something was going to happen that day. The weather was beautiful and sunny; the thunder of the previous night had dwindled to nothing. Some talked about leaving and began to separate out their possessions into what to take and what to leave. One person even buried them in the sand.

I told Martti about such goings-on, and his response was blunt: 'Let everyone else run around: you just stay nice and calm. The others can go if they like. No one really knows what the best chance of survival is, but we're not going anywhere. Anyway, at least for the time being, we've not even been given specific orders to leave.'

But scarcely had those words left his lips when the orders came. The former leader of our brigade – a Karelian man whose wife, daughter and elderly father were with us living in the net hut – arrived from Olonets. He almost ran down the hill and then stopped at the doorway of our shed.

'Here are the permit papers for the evacuation with everybody's names on them. You head towards Lauttajoki, about 18km away. Take just your most essential possessions with you, and only as much as you think you can carry. The situation is extremely precarious. The streets in Olonets are full of refugees. A horse-drawn cart will come to take the children.'

I looked at Martti and met his gaze; I found it somewhat reassuring to hear him calmly and assertively declaring in that deep voice of his, 'Our girl is going with us. I'm not letting her go on the cart. She can run along just as fast as we can with all our belongings. The family stays together.'

The Karelian made a friendly gesture with his hand to imply 'just as you please' and moved along. I sighed deeply and gave my husband a grateful look.

An indescribable pandemonium broke out in the shed. Panicking, everyone was grabbing their belongings and trying to push the most valuable ones into backpacks, sacks or suitcases. Little Rauni was crying and her mother was frozen with a look of agony.

'How am I supposed to get out of here with my baby, all this stuff and the cow?' She said this to no one in particular, surrounded by her belongings while trying to keep her daughter happy. Suddenly the ripping sound of a blast of machine-gun fire was heard.

'Shut the door!' said someone, terrified, whereupon Pirjo's desperate and heart-rending cry was heard from outside the door. The horrified old aunt pushed the door back open and Pirjo and Eva fell in, their faces pale, Pirjo screaming at the old woman. They didn't seem to have come to any harm.

Auntie scolded the children in her own sweet but anxious way: 'Well, what a thing to do! Playing outside at a time like this! In the middle of a war! Inside – that's where you need to be.'

'Oh my God, this is the end,' someone said.

Rauni's mother looked at me with tear-filled eyes: 'Well, Kaarina my dear, what have you got to say now? You always think there's a way out. But it looks like death will come for us all in here, doesn't it?'

'Yes. It does look bad,' I admitted, 'but this isn't the end. Not yet. We just need to keep hoping for a miracle to come and save us.'

So many times already had my long-suffering friends been close to giving up all hope, and here I was still trying to instil courage in them. For the past few years, I had been only able to keep the slenderest hopes alive, feeding and nurturing them. And so I continued even now.

It was almost dark in the shed and someone insisted we should open the door to make it easier to see what we were doing. At that point we were surprised by Pekka, a young unmarried fisherman, limping in, dragging a badly injured leg.

'Oh, Pekka! Have you been shot?'

Pekka limped forward in agony but spoke calmly: 'That's exactly what's happened. It went in at the hip and penetrated my thigh. Is there any chance someone could get some rags to use as a bandage?'

The young girl Erna had by now earned the undisputed position of chief medic in the group. Without delay, she set to, applying the bandages. Loud engine noises were coming from outside; perhaps there were several planes in the vicinity.

'Get up on the edge of the stove, Pirjo!' commanded Martti, as everyone else hunkered down next to the walls. The only one left lying in the middle of the floor was Pekka, teeth gritted and face growing paler.

'You're not managing to tie my bandages,' he said to Erna, who was tinkering helplessly beside him. But neither could anyone else: the horror had robbed everyone of their senses. I was half-naked, and for some reason had pulled on my husband's woollen underwear; Martti was searching in vain for his trousers. I had found the time to dress Pirjo, though.

Pekka remained in the middle of the floor, lying quietly. As if snapping out of a sleep, I realised that I might as well try to bandage his wounds, and at least prevent some of the bleeding. I leaned over to him and took the bandages from Erna. I tied them to the best of my ability, although as I'd never done it before it probably wasn't that great. With Martti's help we got Pekka up. It wasn't easy but we got him outside where there was a horse, harnessed and waiting. In the cart, lying on a stack of hay, was another wounded man – the one who'd given us the permits to flee.

Even the heavens wanted to add to the chaos. The beautiful sunshine of the morning was gone, having retreated to leave a looming black cloud. So just as the wounded were being taken to the village in the hope of medical assistance, heavy rain fell and soaked everything. A mixture of hailstones and rain angrily struck the ground and peppered the flat sandy beach. Someone fetched a rope to tie the wounded more securely to the cart, and I wept as I quietly bid them goodbye, believing it to be the last time I would see them. An old Ingrian man drove the cart.

When I returned to the shed, drenched, the mess was still there. To be fair, some of them were just getting ready to leave and had to jettison anything they couldn't carry. Rauni's mother was crying. She wondered how she could possibly flee, now that the wounded needed the horse and cart that the children were supposed to have.

She looked to me for advice. But an irate Maija cut in bluntly: 'Well, stay here then, if you think you'll make it. It doesn't look like you even want to escape.'

One by one, they managed to make it to the escape route with their cows and their bags until the only ones left in the shed were us. Martti tied a makeshift backpack on each one of us. Pirjo sat by the stove, stiff with fear.

'Well, I guess we at least have to get as far as the forest,' said Martti as he finished what he needed to do.

I agreed, but I still took time to collect my photos. Hurriedly, I detached my favourites, but Martti wasn't rushing me in the slightest, like I thought he would. He just smiled kindly at my peculiar behaviour. It was as if he wanted to stay inside until the last possible minute.

We heard footsteps approaching the shed and we tensed. We had a hunch that the rearguard of the troops would be coming to see if there was anybody left. A frightening thought: would they just shoot us? But it was Rauni and her mother who appeared in the doorway, with Eva and her mother close behind.

Rauni's mother explained: 'It's not worth trying to escape anywhere any more. This commander on horseback came up to me and said it was all too late. According to him the best thing to do is to go and hide in the woods. And I wouldn't have got very far anyway. The bags kept falling off the cow's back and the animal kept acting up. And Rauni's a heavy weight and she won't stop crying. So I turned around and came back, for what it's worth.'

We heard the same from Eva's mother.

I snuck out to explore the situation and around the corner almost ran into an old Karelian woman. She spoke softly to me, and articulated what was in both our hearts: 'Don't hurry so much, sister dear. Where would you poor souls go? On the shores of Russia is starvation and death. Best when you're just here, I guess we will do well, huh!'

I repeated the old lady's words to Martti, which made him keen to go and see what the Karelians in the barracks on top of the hill – with its big, tightly closed doors – had decided to do.

When he returned, he said wryly, 'There's quite a party atmosphere up there. Every last corner is so clean and tidy you'd think they were expecting guests. The belongings were all packed very neatly in a pile, and not a single one of them looked like they were in a hurry to leave. They're just sitting on their long benches along the walls, hands on their laps, waiting.'

It sounded like a complete contrast to our messy shed. But that was only to be expected, as the four families had all got themselves moving, and in the rush their belongings had got mixed up with other people's and strewn across the floor. Just to pass the time, I made a start roughly sorting them all out, with the two women helping. Soon our living quarters were at least in some sort of order.

We heard footsteps again and in came the others. The old couple and Erna entered in a bit of a state, quite full of themselves for some reason. The old woman was so excited that she didn't even bother to sit down but stood there and reeled off her story:

So we walked and walked and walked. I was leading the cow and keeping its load on, my daughter by my side with her father. The others were already far ahead by now. The bags wouldn't stay on the cow's back: they kept sliding down all the time and I kept putting them back on. So we get as far as that berry path – do you remember that path? And then people started pushing past us, young people, old people. Everyone says 'Good morning' all happy and cheerful, and I say the same back. My daughter asks do I know any of these people? Oh no, I don't: that's just the way we always used to greet people in Finland. The girl looks, peers at them, and then says to me, 'Mother, listen! They're ... Finnish soldiers!' Well, if they are, they are – they can't help it. So they then stop and ask us questions and want to know if we're all Finns as well. They were very friendly and seemed very kind. They said not to worry about them. They told us to turn back and they'd leave us in peace, and here we are.

There was another family that had lived with the Karelians in the barracks, even though they were part of our fishing group. They, too, were excited about the people who had told them to turn around.

The girl, Airi, was beaming and said, '... and one officer laughed saying I looked like a blonde Finnish girl. Dad told them we were Finns as well, and that got them talking.'

All this time, the tired Red Army soldiers had been wading across the river, some holding their rifles up against their chest, although many had thrown theirs away. They came in groups or one by one. Looking utterly dejected and harassed, they pushed forward along the shore. Only a few peeked through our shed door but none came inside.

Neither we, nor the Karelians in their barracks, stuck our heads outdoors. We were trying to conceal any signs of life. It wasn't until the cover of darkness that the cows got any attention, and I milked my goat under the big old spruces, where the animals were kept, which was a kind of natural barn. In the early hours of the morning someone came up to our shed and just lay down in the doorway. In the morning light, we could see that he was a young and fit-looking Red soldier. A short time later, a middle-aged Ingrian soldier turned up, his face a complete mess. He had been shot from behind and the bullet had broken several teeth, ripped his cheek muscle and exited through his mouth.

'There's someone else coming,' whispered Pirjo.

A young lad in military uniform, barely 17 years old, crept in, and literally fell to the floor. He'd been shot through the ankle. And yet another soldier arrived. They all seemed to be looking to us for protection. We tried to explain how it would be better for them to find an empty shed somewhere else, but only one of them – a Jewish boy who was in the worst condition of them all – seemed to take our advice seriously, but he was in no condition to take even a single step.

There were passers-by aplenty now. A couple of times someone opened the door, leaned inside and whispered to us urging us to get away. 'You'll be killed if you don't leave' or 'The youth allies are leaving; you need to get out'. But no one left the shed. One person opened out his leg puttees and tied them up again as slowly as possible, just to kill time. The Ingrian, holding a small mirror up, asked for water to clean the blood off his cheek. I couldn't stop myself telling him how awful I thought his wound looked, but the man almost imperceptibly raised his head and replied with no emotion: 'This is nothing. In fact, I could have carried on fighting with this if I'd wanted to. But why would you? It was nothing less than a massacre at Reka Tuloksa.'

Calmly and quietly, he told us his story as he attended to his wound. He had been imprisoned during the Great Purge, too, and sent to a Siberian prison camp. To this day he had no idea why and he hadn't seen it coming. It had been three years of nothing but grey desperation. Then, just a couple of months ago, he had been one of 9,000 prisoners who without warning were put on a train, dressed in uniform and transported to the battle front – an untrained and embittered cohort. The situation that met them at Reka Tuloksa was horrific. Finns fired at them relentlessly and mercilessly, with intermittent calls for surrender blaring from loudspeakers.

'A couple of boys gave it a go, but they ran into a Russian mine. I was thinking about how to get to the other side as well, but you've always got to be wary of bullets coming from your own side. It wasn't much of a laugh, coming out of prison to be turned into cannon fodder. What on earth was I supposed to be fighting for anyway?' Choked with bitterness, he said no more.

We kept someone continually on guard by the tiny, smeared window. It's possible the Finns wouldn't even notice this half-forested coastal road: maybe they'd go straight from the former border guard barracks about 1km from the beach via the barracks road to the village, thus meeting our refugees and turning them back. But we were all highly surprised not to see even any reconnaissance patrols. So we had no way of knowing whose side we were supposed to be on; and that kind of uncertainty was hardly a source of comfort.

The guests finally left our shed and moved on to another, which was already occupied by a wounded, noseless Red soldier. The Jewish boy's foot was so swollen he had to be carried. Time dragged agonisingly while we just waited and listened. Then we all charged out when someone at the door whispered, 'The Finns are coming!'

Indeed, there they were on top of the hill: a small group of serious-looking grey-jacketed soldiers mounted on bicycles. They were currently in talks with the Karelians. They all greeted us kindly – 'Good day! Good day!' I noticed how they were still scanning the surroundings intently, on the lookout for enemy agents. The Red soldiers from the other shed started walking towards the Finns, the Ingrian at the front keeping his hands aloft, seemingly resigned to what was happening. A quick check of their prisoners and the Finnish boys said their goodbyes and returned to the village, hemming the Red soldiers in as they went.

Feeling much more at ease, we returned to our shed. One of us just laughed and said, 'Well, it looks like we're residents of the Republic of Finland again.'

And there it was: who would have believed it? Just think: little Finland defeats its mighty rival. It's a miracle indeed. The children, too, shook off the tension that had shackled them for the last few days; they even dared to go out and play, still a little timidly, though.

37

August 1941

So, yes: we were indeed so much freer now. We felt like we could dare to cook outside once again on our campfires – the first time they'd been ablaze for so long. That evening, we fell asleep in complete peace. The next morning, some Karelian women went with Martti to the village to see what things looked like there – but more importantly to find out what we had to do and if we could get some food. They took the sacks of potatoes with them just in case.

After they'd gone, another commotion broke out in the shed, followed by a rush to the door. More Finns had arrived. There were two of them, standing on top of the hill. The taller one was an officer. He was fair-haired and was leaning on his bike looking benignly at the Karelians grouped around him. Next to him was a young military boy with a permanent grin on his face. I stood at the back of the crowd with a couple of other women. To my total bemusement, the officer, smiling sincerely, put out his hand to greet me. I mumbled something in my embarrassment and looked round to see everyone else being greeted just as warmly. As if picking up from a previous conversation, he said with some conviction, 'Well, you're free from the Russian yoke now. I'm sure you'll all find happiness and contentment before too long.'

Or it was some earnest, serious words of that nature. There was a benevolent smile on his face and his voice was full of warmth and comfort. It was as if a free and joyful springtime had just broken out. I wanted to scream at him and tell him how much I had been waiting just to hear those words – so passionately, so desperately looking for a miracle, having lost all hope except in my dreams.

I wasn't following his words any more; I was just feeling the moment. Intense emotions overwhelmed me. At last, it was good to be alive again and I could breathe easily. Poju flashed through my head. And my parents. Before these thoughts had even finished forming, I spluttered breathlessly, 'Could I ... would I ... be able ... through you ... to let my relatives know that I'm alive ... I'm here and I'm still alive?'

He turned to me and asked, clearly bemused, 'I suppose so, but where's this message going? To hear you speak, you're definitely not locals.'

'No – you're right. I'm from Helsinki originally.' For some reason my voice was timid and quiet.

'Really?! How on earth have you ended up here?' The question was quite straightforward. So straightforward that it ruled out a dishonest or superficial response. The look in his eyes was one of patience not severity, as he waited for a direct answer. Or was that just my interpretation?

Well – yes – what *had* dragged me away from my homeland? Had my character needed building so much that I had to endure nine years of brutal shocks, assaults and pain? After all, I hadn't been driven here by unemployment; I didn't leave home just to find an easier life, whether through chance or adventure. I mean, my conditions had been relatively satisfactory. I left of my own free will: nobody had put any pressure on me. But now, acknowledging the mistakes I had made, did I have to hang my head like a criminal? Or was I just going to wriggle out of answering the question?

No! Never! Everything within me rose up to resist. Let it be known I came here, I endured one intense, brutal blow after another; the work was hard. With death all around me for so many years, I had crept like a shadow, terrified and submissive. I had learned my bitter lesson and paid for my mistake many times over: I could not be held accountable any more. Let me at last breathe deeply and freely once again!

August 1941

There was a feeling in the air that this was a reckoning; yet still I hadn't spoken. Maybe my silence had only lasted a short moment, but to me it was an eternity. I raised my head and met the man's attentive, quizzical eyes. Perhaps he would understand; perhaps he would condemn. Slowly, I said, 'I came here nine years ago, but of my own free will and with a passport. That was who I was then – I won't deny it – but those years have totally changed me and opened my eyes.'

His gaze was intense, and in his voice I heard understanding and belief in what I'd said.

'Is that so? Well, it's a good thing it all became clear to you,' he said with a laugh. And, as if to give me time to calm down, he continued, 'Write whatever you want: I'll be happy to deliver the good news.'

I ran to the shed looking for paper and a pen. Blinded by my tears, I pulled the pen steadily across the page: strong words. But they came from a heart that was warm and sunny – unbound like spring flood waters, revelling in their own power and their joy. The words told of the years of longing for my child and my home – the yearning and the delight at the thought of seeing them again. It's as if I'm already on my way – back to mine, to my home, to my homeland.

Epilogue
by Anna Hyrske

Kaarina's book ends quite abruptly, with no explanation of what happened next or any further information about the fate of the main characters. The person she spoke to in the final paragraphs – whom she entreated to get a message to her family – was, by coincidence, a young man who had attended the same school as my grandfather, 'Poju'. The soldier recognised my grandfather's name on the letter and promised to pass on the information as requested. Happily, the family was indeed reunited. However, the outcome of the war meant that Kaarina couldn't have stayed in Finland in safety. From the Soviet point of view, she wasn't a Finnish citizen, she was a Soviet defector – so she most likely would have suffered the same fate as thousands of other emigrant Finns in Stalin's era. Losing the Continuation War meant that Finland was subject to requirements set forth by the ACC, the overwhelming majority (over 90 per cent) of its members being Soviets. The ACC demanded the return of Soviet citizens, including ethnic minorities, by force if necessary.

After the Winter War of 1939–40, Finland attempted to regain the areas it had conceded. It declared war against the Soviet Union following Red Army air raids on Finnish cities; this was the starting point of the so-called Continuation War (1941–44). The Red Army was simultaneously engaged in another offensive against the Nazis, known as Operation Barbarossa. Finland had an agreement with Germany in which they exchanged data and received training and weapons, in return allowing German troops to enter via Norway to attack the Soviet Union in its northernmost areas. Germany also had its eye on securing access to nickel, a vital raw material, and Finland had a significant mining operation in Lapland; this was of interest not only to Germany but also to Britain and later the Soviet Union.

Although Finland acted as an ally to Nazi Germany, none of its fighters was sent to bomb St Petersburg during Operation Barbarossa; however, Finnish troops were responsible for securing one side of the offensive which amounted to just under 100km of the city's border. Finnish interests lay first and foremost in securing the former borders and regaining their old land. With the offensive going well in the summer of 1941, Finnish troops penetrated further into the Soviet Union – which explains why Kaarina, Martti and Pirjo could see Finnish soldiers passing their hut even after having evacuated from Nukuttalahti to the Soviet side of the border (that is, the border prior to the Winter War).

By summer 1944, the tables were turning, and the Soviets mounted a major counteroffensive. This led to the ceasefire of September 1944. The intermediate peace accord known as the Moscow Armistice required Finland to use military force against any Germans still on Finnish soil by pushing them back to Norway via Lapland. The German troops employed a 'scorched earth' technique and planted landmines, burning and blasting everything as they retreated.

The price of Finland's independence was its agreement to stringent conditions according to the peace accord, which included a Soviet-led monitoring commission stationed on Finnish soil. In addition to the areas already lost after the Winter War,[44] Finland was required to hand over further sections and lease out a significant land mass close to its capital for the use of the Soviet military. Finland suffered a permanent loss of nearly 10 per cent of its land, which included resource-rich

---

44 See map on page 14.

Epilogue by Anna Hyrske

areas and the Petsamo 'panhandle' – its only coastal access to the Arctic Ocean.[45] In addition, it was obliged to pay US$300 million (in 1938 prices[46]) in reparations to the Soviet Union, although this sum was later lowered to US$226.5 million. These reparations were not paid in cash but rather as commodities, such as locomotives, electric motors, ships, wooden houses, machinery and so on. The payment terms were harsh: during the most intensive years, the reparations accounted for around 15–16 per cent of entire government annual expenditure. Furthermore, the payment schedule was extended from six to eight years, meaning that the last train carrying war reparation goods didn't leave Finland until September 1952. Finland is still the only country to have paid its war reparations in full.

To maintain a peaceful relationship, and guarantee its continued independence, Finland complied with the Commission's demands, which included the book censorship programme. Possibly because of this relationship (and because of its high maintenance costs), in 1956 Finland was able to negotiate the early release of the Porkkala coastal area, almost forty years ahead of the lease agreement. This area, just 40km from Helsinki, had been leased out on a fifty-year term to the Soviet Union as part of the peace agreement, its almost 8,000 inhabitants forced to leave the area in a matter of days. The agreement had allowed the Soviets to use it as a military base, with guaranteed rail links to the Soviet Union through Finnish territory. Upon their return, the former inhabitants were greeted with a similar scene to the one Kaarina had witnessed in Nukuttalahti. Buildings had been torn down just for firewood, others had fallen apart from lack of maintenance, or burnt down, or had been otherwise destroyed. Those still standing had been gutted, sometimes with even their fireplaces removed, and taken across the border before the Finns could return. Tombstones had been removed from churchyards and used as building material further down the road. Even though during those eleven years Finns had no access to the area, the Soviets made sure

---

45 See map on page 14.
46 Equivalent to over US$6 *billion* in 2022.

the passenger trains passing through from Helsinki to Turku had steel shutters over their windows to prevent non-Soviets seeing what had become of it. It was generally assumed Porkkala would now boast paved roads, concrete bridges, maybe some grandeur and some style. No. All that greeted them were dirt roads, demolished buildings and the destroyed remains of coastal artillery.

Kaarina never returned to the Soviet Union but lived the remainder of her life in Sweden, where she fled quite soon after finishing this book. Details about how she made it across and who helped her remain unclear to the family to this day. What is known is that she was questioned extensively by the Finnish military before being able to travel back to southern Finland from where she most likely subsequently made her way to Sweden. We also know that, in late September 1944 (after the ceasefire and the arrival of the ACC), she was granted a short-term internal travel permit to go from Helsinki to the west coast of Finland for visiting and work purposes. The permit was applied for just one day before the ACC arrived in Finland and was granted two days later. By January 1945 she was in Sweden.

Poju has three sons, six grandchildren and, at the time of writing, five great-grandchildren. He still lives in Helsinki, only a few blocks from the streets he grew up in. He can see the sea from his living room window; the small islets he stood guard on as a 17-year-old newly recruited soldier are not very far away. In the depth of night, he would scan the dark and stormy sea for submarines – or any other attacking Soviet forces – with nothing but a rifle to defend himself. He considers himself incredibly fortunate: he could very easily have ended up on the Eastern Front. But, as luck would have it, when the young recruits were divided into two groups, he and his best friend were in the one that had more responsibility for the southern sections. His cousin found himself in the other group and never came home. My grandfather says the war forced them to grow up in a single day: the day they traded their milk ration cards for military ones.

Pirjo has a son and a daughter and four grandchildren. She returned from Sweden later in life to be closer to her family. She revisited her childhood home just once after the Communist Party had collapsed

Epilogue by Anna Hyrske

and Russia emerged as a more open society (for a while). Despite having a Swedish passport, her border crossing did not go smoothly. Even a half a century later, her birthplace and background clearly raised some eyebrows among the Russian immigration officers.

Martti did not flee to Sweden but lived out his life quietly in Finland, remaining in contact with Poju's and Pirjo's maternal grandmother.

You may also enjoy ...

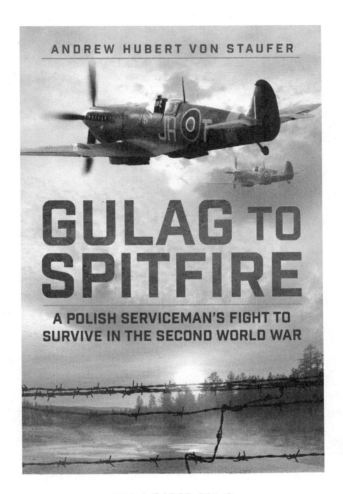

978 1 80399 521 2

The destination for history
www.thehistorypress.co.uk